D0757796

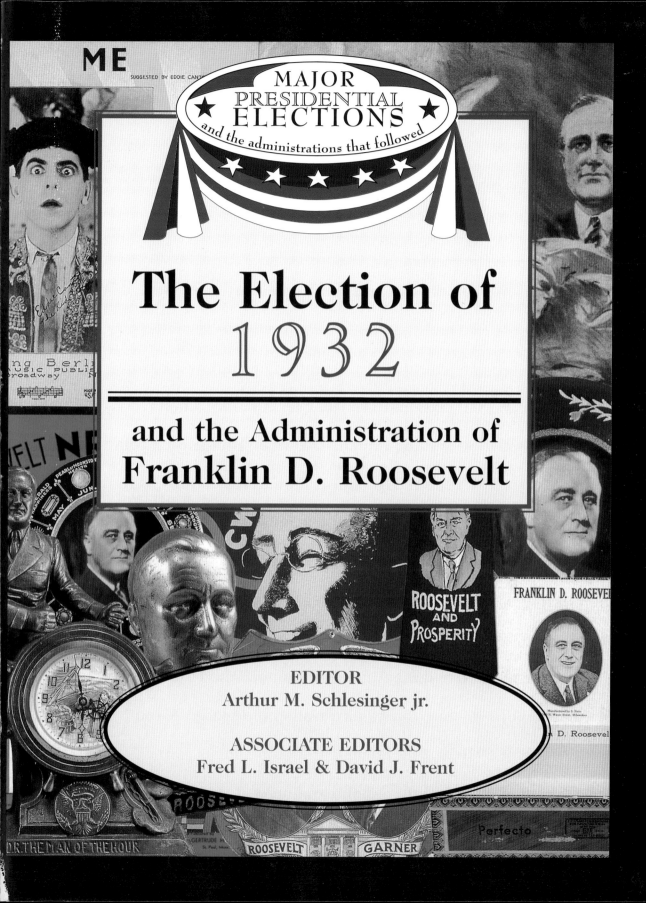

MAJOR PRESIDENTIAL ELECTIONS

and the administrations that followed

The Election of
1932

and the Administration of
Franklin D. Roosevelt

EDITOR
Arthur M. Schlesinger jr.

ASSOCIATE EDITORS
Fred L. Israel & David J. Frent

The Elections of 1789 & 1792 and the Administration of George Washington

The Election of 1800 and the Administration of Thomas Jefferson

The Election of 1828 and the Administration of Andrew Jackson

The Election of 1840 and the Harrison/Tyler Administrations

The Election of 1860 and the Administration of Abraham Lincoln

The Election of 1876 and the Administration of Rutherford B. Hayes

The Election of 1896 and the Administration of William McKinley

The Election of 1912 and the Administration of Woodrow Wilson

The Election of 1932 and the Administration of Franklin D. Roosevelt

The Election of 1948 and the Administration of Harry S. Truman

The Election of 1960 and the Administration of John F. Kennedy

The Election of 1968 and the Administration of Richard Nixon

The Election of 1976 and the Administration of Jimmy Carter

The Election of 1980 and the Administration of Ronald Reagan

The Election of 2000 and the Administration of George W. Bush

MAJOR
PRESIDENTIAL
ELECTIONS
and the administrations that followed

The Election of
1932

and the Administration of Franklin D. Roosevelt

EDITOR

Arthur M. Schlesinger, jr.
Albert Schweitzer Chair in the Humanities
The City University of New York

★

ASSOCIATE EDITORS

Fred L. Israel
Department of History
The City College of New York

David J. Frent
The David J. and Janice L. Frent
Political Americana Collection

Mason Crest Publishers
Philadelphia

Produced by OTTN Publishing, Stockton, New Jersey

Mason Crest Publishers
370 Reed Road
Broomall PA 19008
www.masoncrest.com

Research Consultant: Patrick R. Hilferty
Editorial Assistant: Jane Ziff

First printing

1 3 5 7 9 8 6 4 2

Library of Congress Cataloging-in-Publication Data

The election of 1932 and the administration of Franklin D. Roosevelt / editor, Arthur M. Schlesinger, Jr.; associate editors, Fred L. Israel & David J. Frent.
p. cm. — (Major presidential elections and the administrations that followed)
Summary: A discussion of the presidential election of 1932 and the subsequent administration of Franklin D. Roosevelt, based on source documents.
Includes bibliographical references and index.
ISBN 1-59084-359-2
1. Presidents—United States—Election—1932—Juvenile literature. 2. Presidents—United States—Election—1932—Sources—Juvenile literature 3. Roosevelt, Franklin D. (Franklin Delano), 1882-1945—Juvenile literature. 4. United States—Politics and government—1933-1945—Juvenile literature. 5. United States—Politics and government—1933-1945—Sources—Juvenile literature. [1. Presidents—Election—1932—Sources. 2. Roosevelt, Franklin D. (Franklin Delano), 1882-1945. 3. Elections. 4. United States—Politics and government—1933-1945—Sources.]
I. Schlesinger, Arthur Meier, 1917-   II. Israel, Fred L. III. Frent, David J. IV. Series.
E805 .E44 2003
973.917—dc21

2002012376

Publisher's note: all quotations in this book come from original sources, and contain the spelling and grammatical inconsistencies of the original text.

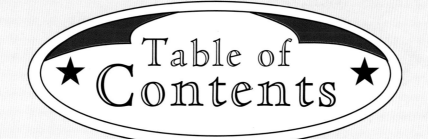

Table of Contents

★ INTRODUCTION ★
Arthur M. Schlesinger, Jr.

America suffers from a sort of intermittent fever—what one may call a quintan ague. Every fourth year there come terrible shakings, passing into the hot fit of the presidential election; then follows what physicians call "the interval"; then again the fit.

—James Bryce, *The American Commonwealth* (1888)

Running for president is the central rite in the American political order. It was not always so. *Choosing* the chief magistrate had been the point of the quadrennial election from the beginning, but it took a long while for candidates to *run* for the highest office in the land; that is, to solicit, visibly and actively, the support of the voters. These volumes show through text and illustration how those aspiring to the White House have moved on from ascetic self-restraint to shameless self-merchandising. This work thereby illuminates the changing ways the American people have conceived the role of their President. I hope it will also recall to new generations some of the more picturesque and endearing dimensions of American politics.

The primary force behind the revolution in campaign attitudes and techniques was a development unforeseen by the men who framed the Constitution—the rise of the party system. Party competition was not at all their original intent. Quite the contrary: inspired at one or two removes by Lord Bolingbroke's British tract of half a century earlier, *The Idea of a Patriot King*, the Founding Fathers envisaged a Patriot President, standing above party and faction, representing the whole people, offering the nation non-partisan leadership virtuously dedicated to the common good.

The ideal of the Patriot President was endangered, the Founding Fathers believed, by twin menaces—factionalism and factionalism's ugly offspring, the demagogue. Party competition would only encourage unscrupulous men to appeal to popular passion and prejudice. Alexander Hamilton in the 71st Federalist bemoaned the plight of the people, "beset as they continually are . . . by the snares of the ambitious, the avaricious, the desperate, by the artifices of men who possess their confidence more than they deserve it, and of those who seek to possess rather than to deserve it."

Pervading the Federalist was a theme sounded explicitly both in the first paper and the last: the fear that unleashing popular passions would bring on "the military despotism of a victorious demagogue." If the "mischiefs of faction" were, James Madison admitted in the Tenth Federalist, "sown in the nature of man," the object of politics was to repress this insidious disposition, not to yield to it. "If I could not go to heaven but with a party," said Thomas Jefferson, "I would not go there at all."

So the Father of his Country in his Farewell Address solemnly warned his countrymen against "the baneful effects of the spirit of party." That spirit, Washington conceded, was "inseparable from our nature"; but for popular government it was "truly their worst enemy." The "alternate domination of one faction over another," Washington said, would lead in the end to "formal and permanent despotism." The spirit of a party, "a fire not to be quenched . . . demands a uniform vigilance to prevent its bursting into a flame, lest, instead of warming, it should consume."

Yet even as Washington called on Americans to "discourage and restrain" the spirit of party, parties were beginning to crystallize around him. The eruption of partisanship in defiance of such august counsel argued that party competition might well serve functional necessities in the democratic republic.

After all, honest disagreement over policy and principle called for candid debate. And parties, it appeared, had vital roles to play in the consummation of the Constitution. The distribution of powers among three equal branches inclined the national government toward a chronic condition of stalemate. Parties offered the means of overcoming the constitutional separation of powers by coordinating the executive and legislative branches and furnishing the connective tissue essential to effective government. As national associations, moreover, parties were a force against provincialism and separatism. As instruments of compromise, they encouraged, within the parties as well as between them, the containment and mediation of national quarrels, at least until slavery broke the parties up. Henry D. Thoreau cared little enough for politics, but he saw the point: "Politics is, as it were, the gizzard of society, full of grit and gravel, and the two political parties are its two opposite halves, which grind on each other."

Furthermore, as the illustrations in these volumes so gloriously remind us, party competition was a great source of entertainment and fun—all the more important in those faraway days before the advent of baseball and football, of movies and radio and television. "To take a hand in the regulation of society and to discuss it," Alexis de Tocqueville observed when he visited America in the 1830s, "is his biggest concern and, so to speak, the only pleasure an American knows. . . . Even the women frequently attend public meetings and listen to political harangues as a recreation from their household labors. Debating clubs are, to a certain extent, a substitute for theatrical entertainments."

Condemned by the Founding Fathers, unknown to the Constitution, parties nonetheless imperiously forced themselves into political life. But the party system rose from the bottom up. For half a century, the first half-dozen Presidents continued to hold themselves above party. The disappearance of the Federalist Party after the War of 1812 suspended party competition. James Monroe, with no opponent at all in the election of 1820, presided proudly over the Era of Good Feelings, so called because there were no parties around to excite ill feelings. Monroe's successor, John Quincy Adams, despised electioneering and inveighed against the "fashion of peddling for popularity by traveling around the country gathering crowds together, hawking for public dinners, and spouting empty speeches." Men of the old republic believed presidential candidates should be men who already deserved the people's confidence rather than those seeking to win it. Character and virtue, not charisma and ambition, should be the grounds for choosing a President.

Adams was the last of the old school. Andrew Jackson, by beating him in the 1828 election, legitimized party politics and opened a new political era. The rationale of the new school was provided by Jackson's counselor and successor, Martin Van Buren, the classic philosopher of the role of party in the American democracy. By the time Van Buren took his own oath of office in 1837, parties were entrenched as the instruments of American self-government. In Van Buren's words, party battles "rouse the sluggish to exertion, give increased energy to the most active intellect, excite a salutary vigilance over our public functionaries, and prevent that apathy which has proved the ruin of Republics."

Apathy may indeed have proved the ruin of republics, but rousing the sluggish to exertion proved, ironically, the ruin of Van Buren. The architect of the party system became the first casualty of the razzle-dazzle campaigning the system quickly generated. The Whigs' Tippecanoe-and-Tyler-too campaign of 1840 transmuted the democratic Van Buren into a gilded aristocrat and assured his defeat at the polls. The "peddling for popularity" John Quincy Adams had deplored now became standard for party campaigners.

But the new methods were still forbidden to the presidential candidates themselves. The feeling lingered from earlier days that stumping the country in search of votes was demagoguery beneath the dignity of the presidency. Van Buren's code permitted—indeed expected—parties to inscribe their creed in platforms and candidates to declare their principles in letters published in newspapers. Occasionally candidates—William Henry Harrison in 1840, Winfield Scott in 1852—made a speech, but party surrogates did most of the hard work.

As late as 1858, Van Buren, advising his son John, one of the great popular orators of the time, on the best way to make it to the White House, emphasized the "rule . . . that the people will never make a man President who is so importunate as to show by his life and conversation that he not only has an eye on, but is in active pursuit of the office. . . . No man who has laid himself out for it, and was unwise enough to let the people into his secret, ever yet obtained it. Clay, Calhoun, Webster, Scott, and a host of lesser lights, should serve as a guide-post to future aspirants."

The continuing constraint on personal campaigning by candidates was reinforced by the desire of party managers to present their nominees as all things to all men. In 1835 Nicholas Biddle, the wealthy Philadelphian who had been Jackson's mortal opponent in the famous Bank War, advised the Whigs not to let General Harrison "say one single word about his principles or his creed. . . . Let him say nothing, promise nothing. Let no committee, no convention, no town meeting ever extract from him a single word about what he thinks now, or what he will do hereafter. Let the use of pen and ink be wholly forbidden as if he were a mad poet in Bedlam."

We cherish the memory of the famous debates in 1858 between Abraham Lincoln and Stephen A. Douglas. But those debates were not part of a presidential election. When the presidency was at stake two years later, Lincoln gave no campaign speeches on the issues darkly dividing the country. He even expressed doubt about party platforms—"the formal written platform system," as he called it. The candidate's character and record, Lincoln thought, should constitute his platform: "On just such platforms all our earlier and better Presidents were elected."

However, Douglas, Lincoln's leading opponent in 1860, foreshadowed the future when he broke the sound barrier and dared venture forth on thinly disguised campaign tours. Yet Douglas established no immediate precedent. Indeed, half a dozen years later Lincoln's successor, Andrew Johnson, discredited presidential stumping by his "swing around the circle" in the midterm election of 1866. "His performances in a western tour in advocacy of his own election," commented Benjamin F. Butler, who later led the fight in Congress for Johnson's impeachment, ". . . disgusted everybody." The tenth article of impeachment charged Johnson with bringing "the high office of the President of the United States into contempt, ridicule, and disgrace" by delivering "with a loud voice certain intemperate, inflammatory, and scandalous harangues . . . peculiarly indecent and unbecoming in the Chief Magistrate of the United States."

Though presidential candidates Horatio Seymour in 1868, Rutherford B. Hayes in 1876, and James A. Garfield in 1880 made occasional speeches, only Horace Greeley in 1872, James G. Blaine in 1884, and most spectacularly, William Jennings Bryan in 1896 followed Douglas's audacious example of stumping the country. Such tactics continued to provoke disapproval. Bryan, said John Hay, who had been Lincoln's private secretary and was soon to become McKinley's secretary of state, "is begging for the presidency as a tramp might beg for a pie."

Respectable opinion still preferred the "front porch" campaign, employed by Garfield, by Benjamin Harrison in 1888, and most notably by McKinley in 1896. Here candidates received and addressed numerous delegations at their own homes—a form, as the historian Gil Troy writes, of "stumping in place."

While candidates generally continued to stand on their dignity, popular campaigning in presidential elections flourished in these years, attaining new heights of participation (82 percent of eligible voters in 1876 and never once from 1860 to 1900 under 70 percent) and new wonders of pyrotechnics and ballyhoo. Parties mobilized the electorate as never before, and political iconography was never more ingenious and fantastic. "Politics, considered not as the science of government, but as the art of winning elections and securing office," wrote the keen British observer James Bryce, "has reached in the United States a development surpassing in elaborateness that of England or France as much as the methods of those countries surpass the methods of

Servia or Roumania." Bryce marveled at the "military discipline" of the parties, at "the demonstrations, the parades and receptions, the badges and brass bands and triumphal arches," at the excitement stirred by elections—and at "the disproportion that strikes a European between the merits of the presidential candidate and the blazing enthusiasm which he evokes."

Still the old taboo held back the presidential candidates themselves. Even so irrepressible a campaigner as President Theodore Roosevelt felt obliged to hold his tongue when he ran for reelection in 1904. This unwonted abstinence reminded him, he wrote in considerable frustration, of the July day in 1898 when he was "lying still under shell fire" during the Spanish-American War. "I have continually wished that I could be on the stump myself."

No such constraint inhibited TR, however, when he ran again for the presidency in 1912. Meanwhile, and for the first time, *both* candidates in 1908—Bryan again, and William Howard Taft—actively campaigned for the prize. The duties of the office, on top of the new requirements of campaigning, led Woodrow Wilson to reflect that same year, four years before he himself ran for President, "Men of ordinary physique and discretion cannot be Presidents and live, if the strain be not somehow relieved. We shall be obliged always to be picking our chief magistrates from among wise and prudent athletes,—a small class."

Theodore Roosevelt and Woodrow Wilson combined to legitimate a new conception of presidential candidates as active molders of public opinion in active pursuit of the highest office. Once in the White House, Wilson revived the custom, abandoned by Jefferson, of delivering annual state of the union addresses to Congress in person. In 1916 he became the first incumbent President to stump for his own reelection.

The activist candidate and the bully-pulpit presidency were expressions of the growing democratization of politics. New forms of communication were reconfiguring presidential campaigns. In the nineteenth century the press, far more fiercely partisan then than today, had been the main carrier of political information. In the twentieth century the spread of advertising techniques and the rise of the electronic media—radio, television, computerized public opinion polling—wrought drastic changes in the methodology of politics. In particular the electronic age diminished and now threatens to dissolve the historic role of the party.

The old system had three tiers: the politician at one end; the voter at the other; and the party in between. The party's function was to negotiate between the politician and the voters, interpreting each to the other and providing the link that held the political process together. The electric revolution has substantially abolished the sovereignty of the party. Where once the voter turned to the local party leader to find out whom to support, now he looks at television and makes up his own mind. Where once the politician turned to the local party leader to find out what people are thinking, he now takes a computerized poll.

The electronic era has created a new breed of professional consultants, "handlers," who by the 1980s had taken control of campaigns away from the politicians. The traditional pageantry—rallies, torchlight processions, volunteers, leaflets, billboards, bumper stickers—is now largely a thing of the past. Television replaces the party as the means of mobilizing the voter. And as the party is left to wither on the vine, the presidential candidate becomes more pivotal than ever. We shall see the rise of personalist movements, founded not on historic organizations but on compelling personalities, private fortunes, and popular frustrations. Without the stabilizing influence of parties, American politics would grow angrier, wilder, and more irresponsible.

Things have changed considerably from the austerities of the old republic. Where once voters preferred to call presumably reluctant candidates to the duties of the supreme magistracy and rejected pursuit of the office as evidence of dangerous ambition, now they expect candidates to come to them, explain their views and plead for their support. Where nonpartisan virtue had been the essence, now candidates must prove to voters that they have the requisite "fire in the belly." "'Twud be inth'restin," said Mr. Dooley, ". . . if th' fathers iv th' counthry cud come back an' see what has happened while they've been away. In times past whin ye voted f'r president ye didn't vote f'r a man. Ye voted f'r a kind iv a statue that ye'd put up in ye'er own mind on a marble pidistal. Ye nivir heerd iv George Wash'nton goin' around th' counthry distributin' five cint see-gars."

We have reversed the original notion that ambition must be disguised and the office seek the man. Now the man—and soon, one must hope, the woman— seeks the office and does so without guilt or shame or inhibition. This is not necessarily a degradation of democracy. Dropping the disguise is a gain for candor, and personal avowals of convictions and policies may elevate and educate the electorate.

On the other hand, the electronic era has dismally reduced both the intellectual content of campaigns and the attention span of audiences. In the nineteenth century political speeches lasted for a couple of hours and dealt with issues in systematic and exhaustive fashion. Voters drove wagons for miles to hear Webster and Clay, Bryan and Teddy Roosevelt, and felt cheated if the famous orator did not give them their money's worth. Then radio came along and cut political addresses down first to an hour, soon to thirty minutes—still enough time to develop substantive arguments.

But television has shrunk the political talk first to fifteen minutes, now to the sound bite and the thirty-second spot. Advertising agencies today sell candidates with all the cynical contrivance they previously devoted to selling detergents and mouthwash. The result is the debasement of American politics. "The idea that you can merchandise candidates for high office like breakfast cereal," Adlai Stevenson said in 1952, "is the ultimate indignity to the democratic process."

Still Bryce's "intermittent fever" will be upon us every fourth year. We will continue to watch wise if not always prudent athletes in their sprint for the White House, enjoy the quadrennial spectacle and agonize about the outcome.

"The strife of the election," said Lincoln after his reelection in 1864, "is but human-nature practically applied to the facts. What has occurred in this case, must ever recur in similar cases. Human-nature will not change."

Lincoln, as usual, was right. Despite the transformation in political methods there remains a basic continuity in political emotions. "For a long while before the appointed time has come," Tocqueville wrote more than a century and a half ago, "the election becomes the important and, so to speak, the all-engrossing topic of discussion. Factional ardor is redoubled, and all the artificial passions which the imagination can create in a happy and peaceful land are agitated and brought to light. . . .

"As the election draws near, the activity of intrigue and the agitation of the populace increase; the citizens are divided into hostile camps, each of which assumes the name of its favorite candidate; the whole nation glows with feverish excitement; the election is the daily theme of the press, the subject of every private conversation, the end of every thought and every action, the sole interest of the present.

"It is true," Tocqueville added, "that as soon as the choice is determined, this ardor is dispelled, calm returns, and the river, which had nearly broken its banks, sinks to its usual level; but who can refrain from astonishment that such a storm should have arisen?"

The election storm in the end blows fresh and clean. With the tragic exception of 1860, the American people have invariably accepted the result and given the victor their hopes and blessings. For all its flaws and follies, democracy abides.

Let us now turn the pages and watch the gaudy parade of American presidential politics pass by in all its careless glory.

The Election of 1932

Frank Freidel was Warren Professor of American History, Emeritus, Harvard University, and Bullitt Professor of American History, Emeritus, University of Washington. Among his books are *Franklin D. Roosevelt* (four volumes, 1952–1973); *FDR and the South* (1965); and a one-volume biography, *Franklin D. Roosevelt: A Rendezvous with Destiny* (1990). Freidel served as president of the Organization of American Historians.

The election of 1932, which swept Franklin Roosevelt into the White House, was an emphatic protest against the Great Depression. Few of the voters could have been aware that it was also the fanfare for one of the most fruitful eras of reform and modernization in American history. Roosevelt, the Democratic challenger, established himself as an exceptionally adroit and innovative campaigner. He astutely offered few specifics of his blueprint for a New Deal, uniting diverse supporters with pledges of action. President Herbert Hoover, earlier hailed as a great engineer and humanitarian, had become the symbol of the old order. Hoover was the issue in 1932, Roosevelt pointed out to his advisers. For his part, Hoover was orthodox in campaigning, as he warned the nation of disasters ahead if it were to abandon the prudent course he had set.

Four years earlier, Hoover, the exponent of prosperity through self-reliance, or "rugged individualism," won by an overwhelming margin, but he had become the scapegoat for the deepening depression. He was sensitive and reserved, no favorite of either the Congress or the reporters, one of whom observed that Hoover was ungenerous to a fault. A joke went the rounds of the Senate in May 1932 that Hoover had been kidnapped. The ransom note read, "If we do not receive $500,000 within two hours, we'll bring him back."

Hoover had been bolder than any previous president in combatting a depression, but his measures—a crop purchase program and the Reconstruction Finance Corporation (which made emergency loans, mostly to large banks and corporations)—were too limited to stimulate effective recovery. In June 1932, as the conventions were about to meet, Hoover urged an uncooperative Congress to vote a manufacturers' excise tax, comparable to present-day value-added taxes.

In November 1928, newspapers suggested that Roosevelt, elected

Poster for Roosevelt's 1930 New York State gubernatorial reelection campaign.

RE-ELECT
GOVERNOR

★ ★

FRANKLIN D.
ROOSEVELT
KEEP PROGRESSIVE GOVERNMENT

governor of New York despite the Hoover landslide, was the prime candidate for the 1932 Democratic nomination. It seemed at the time an empty honor, but the depression transformed the nomination into a coveted prize. Roosevelt had come a long way since 1921 when polio deprived him of the use of his legs, apparently ruling him out of high office. Previously he had been Wilson's assistant secretary of the navy and Democratic vice presidential candidate in 1920. In the 1920s, out of competition, he was a premature "elder statesman" seeking to mend the rift in the Democratic Party between the "wet" Catholic wing (centered in eastern cities) and the "dry" Protestant Democrats in the South and West. His wife, Eleanor, became a skilled political surrogate, and his alter ego Louis McHenry Howe developed an expanding correspondence and publicity schemes to build support. In 1938, Emil Ludwig, a biographer, asked Roosevelt when he had first thought of the presidency. "I, never!" parried Roosevelt, "but Louis Howe never forgot."

When he ran for governor, Roosevelt successfully created the illusion that he was lame, not a paraplegic. With braces on his legs, with a cane in one hand, and with the other grasping the arm of a son or aide, he could move slowly to a rostrum. Newspapers published no embarrassing photographs; that would have been considered unsporting, and Roosevelt, fit and dynamic, was obviously in excellent health. Al Smith, the 1928 Democratic presidential candidate who had persuaded Roosevelt to run for governor, gave the definite response to doubters: "You don't have to be an acrobat to be governor." Or, as Smith later discovered, for Roosevelt to be a contender for the presidency.

As governor, Roosevelt long denied he was eyeing the White House, but after he won reelection in 1930 by a wide margin, he was in all but name a candidate. Howe's letter-writing and fund-raising operation became known as the "Friends of Roosevelt." James A. Farley, the indefatigable chairman of the New York Democratic Committee, was a "political drummer," selling support for Roosevelt throughout the nation. Roosevelt, in response to the depression crisis demonstrated his qualities as an innovator by establishing a state relief agency, model for the subsequent New Deal program, and advocated large-scale action to restore the economy.

In the spring of 1932, with Roosevelt the front-runner by a wide margin, Al Smith announced his candidacy and drew strong support from conservative Democrats. Many of them hoped, after using Smith to stop Roosevelt, to nominate Newton D. Baker (who had been Wilson's secretary of war). The most persistent criticism of Roosevelt was that he had failed to take action against Mayor James Walker and corrupt members of the Tammany machine in New York City. To do so might have cost Roosevelt the nomination. Reformers denounced him as a straddler, amiable but superficial. Walter Lippmann made the most telling attack: "Franklin D. Roosevelt is no crusader. . . . He is a pleasant man who, without any important qualifications for the office, would very much like to be President." President Hoover and his counselors thought Roosevelt the weakest of the Democratic candidates and hoped for his nomination.

When the Republican convention met in Chicago in mid-June 1932,

Poster for Hoover's reelection. Paper items were the dominant ephemera of the 1932 presidential campaign.

Hoover's managers maintained tight control over the dispirited delegates. The platform endorsed Hoover's economic measures, and the keynoter proclaimed that without "that stalwart American," the depression would have been much worse. In nominating him, Representative Joseph L. Scott declared that Hoover "has taught us to strain our individual selves to the limit rather than cowardly to lie down under a paternal government." There was some slight stirring against the dull, conservative vice-president, Charles Curtis, notable only for his Indian ancestors, but the delegates contentedly gave Hoover the daunting task of seeking reelection. The Democratic convention, meeting in Chicago later in June, was more tense and uncertain than the campaign that followed. Roosevelt had more than a majority of the delegates but sixty-six less than the two-thirds required for nomination. Conservative Democrats in alliance with urban bosses might, under the banner of Smith, stop Roosevelt, then consolidate the convention behind a compromise candidate, probably Baker. Smith, who wanted the nomination for himself, was not disposed to be a stalking horse for any other candidate, and he launched his attack against Roosevelt. As the convention assembled, the Smith mimeograph machines poured out copies of a Heywood Brown column vilifying "Feather Duster" Roosevelt, the "cork-screw candidate."

Roosevelt's candidacy was touch and go. The struggle began when Roosevelt supporters opened a drive to eliminate the venerable two-thirds rule. Opposition was so clamorous that Roosevelt decided not to push the challenge. Next came a nasty clash over the election of a Roosevelt adherent, Senator Thomas J. Walsh, to serve as permanent chairman of the

The Republican campaign stressed that only a Republican administration could bring back prosperity.

convention. Opponents accused Roosevelt of bad faith, since earlier he had promised with a weasel word to "commend" Jouett Shouse, a conservative who could have been expected to rule against Roosevelt at critical junctures.

The crucial test of strength came with the balloting for the nomination. For hours in the steaming convention hall extravagant nominating speeches and lengthy demonstrations went on and on while the managers of the candidates tried successfully to negotiate deals to switch delegates. The galleries were packed with vociferous Smith supporters. It was 4:28 on the morning of July 1 when the first balloting began. Farley held a few votes back, and Roosevelt received 666, only 104 short of the nomination. At 9:15 A.M., after two more ballots, he was still 88 short. As the convention recessed until evening, opponents predicted Roosevelt would crack on the next ballot.

Throughout the day, still going without sleep, managers engaged in deal-making. Many of those involved even peripherally claimed later that they had been responsible for the dramatic outcome. The key figure was Speaker John Nance Garner of Texas, whose views were closer to Roosevelt's than those of the opposition. He had no interest in a stalemate. Farley conferred with Garner's

Ceramic pitcher manufactured by the Stangl Co. with caricature of Roosevelt.

manager, Sam Rayburn, who phoned Garner. "Hell," said Garner, "I'll do anything to see the Democrats win one more national election." He agreed to release the Texas delegation and to placate them by accepting nomination for the vice presidency. The publisher, William Randolph Hearst, opposed to the internationalist Baker, backed the switch of the California delegates for Garner. When the convention reconvened, the shift of Garner votes to Roosevelt brought his nomination on the fourth ballot. Smith refused to release his delegates to make the nomination unanimous, but the struggle led to no disruption in the Democratic Party.

Tradition, dating back to the days of stagecoaches, prescribed that some weeks later a delegation would make a formal call upon the nominee and that he would respond with an acceptance address. Roosevelt, demonstrating the dynamism that his wife's Uncle Teddy had made famous, broke with tradition and announced he would accept the nomination before the convention. Much as he disliked flying, Roosevelt had arranged weeks in advance for an airliner to bring him from Albany to Chicago. Against strong headwinds the plane bumped along for nine hours en route, but Roosevelt emerged grinning into a crush that knocked off his glasses.

Radio enabled the nation to follow his flight and to hear his acceptance address. It was a broad array of progressive promises, as attractive to many Republicans as it was to Democrats—drastic government economy, crop limitations to raise farm prices, regulation of securities markets, refinancing of mortgages, and relief for the needy. In his peroration he declared, "I pledge you, I pledge myself, to a new deal for the American people." The term "new deal" was commonplace. But the next day a political cartoon by Rollin Kirby depicted a farmer gazing up at an airplane emblazoned "New Deal." FDR's use of

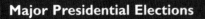

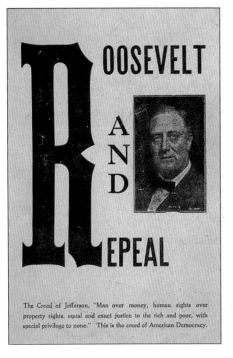

Both sides of the Prohibition issue were expressed on a variety of novelties. The tin tray (right) shows the three little pigs enjoying beer while an Andrew J. Volstead caricature of the big bad wolf threatens them. Congressman Volstead drafted the Prohibition Amendment (1919).

the term had caught the popular fancy.

Roosevelt, although serious obstacles faced him, acted as though he were certain of victory. Powerful party leaders had been aligned against him; much of the better informed electorate agreed with Lippman that Roosevelt was charming but weak, as seen in his failure to cope with Tammany. A few intellectuals found the Socialist candidate, Norman Thomas, more attractive. Campaign funds were also a problem in that depression year; the Democrats had difficulty in raising $1.5 million, although Roosevelt's goal was only a quarter of that of 1928.

President Hoover was disheartened despite reassurances from advisers that Americans, fundamentally conservative, would bury Roosevelt as they had William Jennings Bryan. He steered his campaign along traditional lines trying without much success to appear informal in photographs—riding on horseback and fishing for trout at his previously off-limits hide-away in Virginia. His acceptance address of mid-August warned against experimentation (which Roosevelt had advocated in the spring) and praised his own prudent measures. The nation must turn a deaf ear to

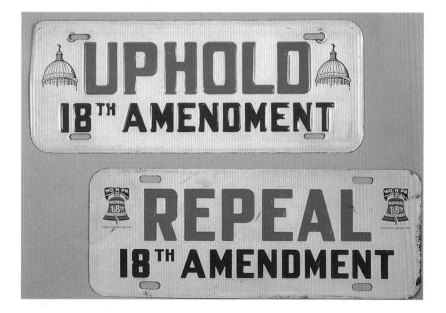

(Left) Paper poster for Pennsylvania Republican rally. (Below) Celluloid button for Hoover and Curtis.

demagogues and slogans. The speech was more graceful and forceful than had been expected. One listener wired, "Rivaled Lincoln at Gettysburg."

At about the same time, an upturn of stock and commodity prices in a "baby bull market," provided an interlude of optimism for Hoover, who decided, in keeping with the dignity of his office, to defer major campaign speeches until October. Republicans began to refer to the depression in the past tense, but few if any economic gains trickled down to the millions in economic peril.

Hoover's unpopularity increased. In August, Milo Reno in Iowa proclaimed a farm strike: "Stay at Home—Sell Nothing." More damaging was the reaction when Hoover directed the Army to remove from Washington 11,000 World War I veterans seeking early payment of a service bonus. Before newsreel cameras, General Douglas MacArthur turned the eviction into a drama. Tanks and soldiers wearing gas masks and fixed bayonets drove the Bonus marchers out of their makeshift hovels. Across the nation irate veterans stood at traffic lights selling "Hoover whistles" which made a raspberry noise, and shanty towns on dumps and along railroad tracks bore the name "Hooverville."

Meanwhile Roosevelt was making detailed preparations for an extensive campaign. Late on the night of his acceptance speech in Chicago, he was outlining speech topics and even contents to Raymond Moley, the head of his "Brains Trust." Unlike Hoover, the last President entirely to write his own speeches, Roosevelt long since had assembled a team that was both expert on issues and skilled at speechwriting. He labored with them painstakingly, reassessing and revising, and always himself writing the perorations—"snappers" he called them.

Farley, who with Roosevelt's nomination had become chairman of the Democratic National Committee, extended nationally the techniques he had used in building the Democratic Party in upstate New York. He sent bundles of campaign literature and posters to county and precinct workers, and gave them recognition through letters, each bearing his signature in distinctive green ink.

The effective participation of women in the campaign, Farley estimated, increased the Democratic vote as much as 10 to 20 percent. Mary ("Molly") Dewson, who had been effective in New York, established a strong national division of the Democratic Party. Women campaigners, Farley noted, "took their jobs in deadly earnest" and were "more faithful . . . in distributing literature . . . and other little irksome tasks."

Both the Democrats and Republicans issued pamphlets, and of course, traditional campaign buttons and insignia, including covers to put on the spare tires carried on the running boards or rear of automobiles. The largest expenditures were upon campaign tours and radio

Pocket mirror for Roosevelt with a colorful birthstone motif.

time. The Republicans, raising about a half-million dollars more than the Democrats, spent more heavily on national broadcasts, purchasing 70 hours for $437,000. There was no cost at all for one of the most influential of the media, the newsreels in which candidates, rallies, and parades appeared before movie-going millions.

Both Democratic and Republican campaigns focused upon the other's candidate for President. While Roosevelt strategy was to emphasize Hoover's failure to remedy the depression, the Republicans from the outset portrayed Roosevelt as a weak nonentity with a leaning toward socialism. Newspapers helped spread the image. The *New York Post* suspected that he lacked "both conscience and intelligence," and the *New York Times* deemed him indefinite and irresolute.

Roosevelt erased doubts of his decisiveness and character by settling the unfinished business with Mayor Walker of New York City. In August he summoned Walker to Albany to answer charges of corruption. Day after day for long hours Roosevelt interrogated Walker in acute, relentless fashion until suddenly on September 1 Walker resigned. Tammanyites were resentful, but, when they tried to punish Roosevelt's lieutenant governor, Smith joined Roosevelt to block Tammany. The two rivals were reconciled, at least temporarily, and Smith

Oilcloth spare-tire covers. Spare tires were mounted on the rear or side of an automobile and were highly visible.

helped win eastern voters to the ticket. Nationally, Roosevelt began to appear strong and masterful.

While campaigning was the favorite sport of Roosevelt— smiling, outgoing, and energetic—to Hoover (who disliked crowds) it was a distasteful task and he appeared fatigued, grim, and dull. In September, after the Democrats won state offices in Maine, Hoover reluctantly agreed to a lengthy tour as far as California. Roosevelt, in contrast, against the recommendation of Farley and Howe insisted upon entraining on a wide sweep of the West. He fol-

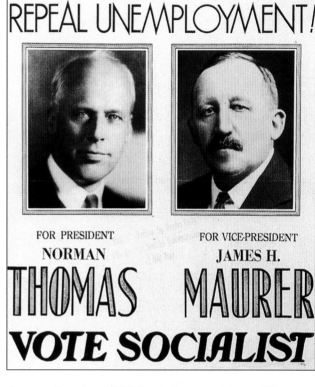

Poster for the 1932 Socialist candidates. They received 2.2 percent of the popular vote.

lowed it with a tour of the South, safely Democratic, where, presumably looking beyond the election he could build support among voters and politicians for future programs.

Roosevelt particularly enjoyed campaigning by train. Cheerful, chatty, and appearing in fine health, he did much to counter rumors that he was too crippled to serve as president. Nor did he always try to hide his condition. At Seattle, he visited crippled children at a hospital and remarked to them, "It's a little difficult for me to stand on my feet too." But on the rear platform of the Pullman car *Pioneer*, on the arm of his six-foot-three son James, polio seemed irrelevant.

"This is my little boy Jimmy," he would begin, eliciting a laugh. Between stops as the six-car train rolled along slowly, he would renew ties with local politicians or work on speeches.

Each of Roosevelt's major campaign speeches dealt with a specific issue in an interesting but not always enlightening way as he moved to left or right to occupy the middle ground. His farm address at Topeka, Kansas, could be seen as favoring several different agricultural recovery programs and was so general that it did not alarm the East. On the tariff he so equivocated that Hoover compared him to a chameleon on plaid, and warned that if Roosevelt were elected, "grass will grow in the streets of a hundred cities." On electric power, he was specific, favoring regulation and some government production of power to act as a yardstick for the measurement of private rates.

Overall, Roosevelt was vigorous in his attack upon the Hoover administration. Late in the campaign he denounced the Republican leadership as the four "Horseman of Destruction, Delay, Deceit, Despair." The Republicans controlled the Congress, the presidency, and, he ad libbed, the Supreme Court. Hoover denounced the remark on the Supreme Court as atrocious. "Does he expect the Supreme Court to be subservient to him and his party?"

Hoover's nine omnibus speeches were variations on the theme that without the Republicans the depression would have been worse. There was little that fall to

(Left) A 1932 satirical campaign book. (Opposite) Toby mug with a smiling Roosevelt.

encourage him or his audiences. Shortly before he spoke in Des Moines, Iowa, Reno and the farm strikers paraded through the streets with signs, "In Hoover we trusted; now we are busted." Republicans assembling to hear the president yelled, "Give 'em hell, Hoover." But the president's delivery was, *Time* taunted, singsong monotony broken by an occasional tremulous note. As election day approached, Hoover became more strident in sounding an alarm. At Madison Square Garden he scoffed at the "new deal" as a "new shuffle" of cards and warned, "this campaign is a contest between two philosophies of government."

Roosevelt, who had stumped 17,000 miles, a record at that time, was far in the lead, and concluded his campaign by summing up his impressions of the countless people he had seen. They had not all agreed with him, he said, but they had all been kind and tolerant. Out of their unity he hoped to fabricate the strongest strand to lift the nation out of the depression.

The election results were as decisive as the straw polls had indicated. Roosevelt received 22,800,000 votes to 15,750,000 for Hoover (57.4 percent to 39.7 percent), and carried 42 states with 472 electoral votes, compared with 6 states and 59 electoral votes for Hoover.

What Roosevelt had offered the voters seemed reminiscent of earlier progressivism, but he had avoided divisions within his party and had won the support of numerous progressive Republicans, onetime adherents of Theodore Roosevelt and Robert M. La Follette. He had received a firm national mandate for change. He was to make full use of it.

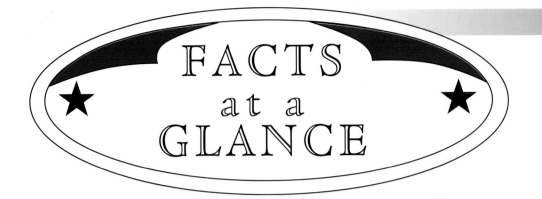

FACTS at a GLANCE

FRANKLIN DELANO ROOSEVELT

- **Born:** January 30, 1882, in Hyde Park, New York
- **Parents:** James and Sara Delano Roosevelt
- **Education:** Graduated from Harvard College in 1903; attended Columbia Law School
- **Occupation:** public official
- **Married:** Anna Eleanor Roosevelt (1884–1962) on March 17, 1905
- **Children:** Anna Eleanor Roosevelt (1906–75); James Roosevelt (1907–91); Elliott Roosevelt (1910–90); Franklin Roosevelt, Jr. (1914–88); John Roosevelt (1916–81)
- **Died:** April 12, 1945, in Warm Springs, Georgia

Served as the 32ND PRESIDENT OF THE UNITED STATES,

- March 4, 1933, to April 12, 1945

VICE PRESIDENT
- John Nance Garner (1933–41)
- Henry A. Wallace (1941–45)
- Harry S. Truman (1945)

CABINET

Secretary of State
- Cordell Hull (1933–44)
- Edward R. Stettinius, Jr. (1944–45)

Secretary of the Treasury
- William H. Woodin (1933–34)
- Henry Morgenthau, Jr. (1934–45)

Secretary of War
- George H. Dern (1933–36)
- Harry H. Woodring (1937–40)
- Henry L. Stimson (1940–45)

Attorney General
- Homer S. Cummings (1933–39)
- Frank Murphy (1939–40)
- Robert H. Jackson (1940–41)
- Francis B. Biddle (1941–45)

Postmaster General
- James A. Farley (1933–40)
- Frank C. Walker (1940–45)

Secretary of the Navy
- Claude A. Swanson (1933–39)
- Charles Edison (1940)
- Frank Knox (1940–44)
- James V. Forrestal (1944–45)

Secretary of the Interior
- Harold L. Ickes (1933–45)

Secretary of Agriculture
- Henry A. Wallace (1933–40)
- Claude R. Wickard (1940–45)

Secretary of Commerce
- Daniel C. Roper (1933–38)
- Harry L. Hopkins (1939–40)
- Jesse H. Jones (1940–45)
- Henry A. Wallace (1945)

Secretary of Labor
- Frances Perkins (1933–1945)

OTHER POLITICAL POSITIONS

- Member of New York State Legislature, 1911–13
- Assistant Secretary of the Navy, 1913–20
- Governor of New York, 1929–33

NOTABLE EVENTS DURING ROOSEVELT'S ADMINISTRATION

1933   Franklin D. Roosevelt is sworn in as president on March 4; pronounces a "bank holiday" March 6–9; sends "Hundred Days" legislation to Congress; the Twentieth Amendment, which changes inauguration day to January; is ratified; the Twenty-first Amendment, which repeals the Eighteenth Amendment (Prohibition) is ratified.

1935   The Social Security Act is passed by Congress; the United States drafts neutrality legislation.

1936   FDR easily wins reelection over Alf Landon.

1937   Roosevelt attempts to pack the Supreme Court.

1939   On September 1, World War II begins in Europe.

1940   Roosevelt trades 50 American warships to Great Britain for the right to establish naval bases on British possessions in the Atlantic; France falls to Nazi Germany; Roosevelt becomes the first president elected to a third term, defeating Wendell Willkie.

1941   The Lend-Lease program is established; Roosevelt and Churchill release the Atlantic Charter; on December 7, Japan attacks the U.S. naval base at Pearl Harbor, leading the United States to enter World War II.

1942   Japanese Americans are interned; American naval forces stop the Japanese at the battles of Coral Sea and Midway.

1944   Allied forces invade Normandy on D-Day (June 6, 1944); U.S. begins bombing Japan; Roosevelt wins fourth term, defeating Thomas E. Dewey.

1945   Roosevelt, Winston Churchill, and Joseph Stalin meet at Yalta; on April 12, Roosevelt dies at Warm Springs, Georgia; Harry S. Truman is sworn in as president; Germany surrenders on May 8; in August, atomic bombs are dropped on the Japanese cities of Hiroshima and Nagasaki, and Japan surrenders, ending World War II.

Anxiety about the Great Depression and dissatisfaction with the policies of incumbent president Herbert Hoover contributed greatly to Franklin D. Roosevelt's victory in 1932. Roosevelt received 22.8 million votes (57.4 percent) and 472 electoral votes to Hoover's 15.75 million votes (39.7 percent) and 59 electoral votes—all from the northeast. The Socialist candidate, Norman Thomas, received about 2.2 percent of the popular vote nationally.

★ Roosevelt Accepts the Nomination ★

Franklin D. Roosevelt, governor of New York, won the Democratic Party's 1932 presidential nomination on the fourth ballot. Roosevelt had cleverly bridged the gulf between the urban and rural delegates. He was ready to emphasize economic issues and ignore the earlier party divisions over prohibition and religion. Breaking precedent, the 50-year-old governor flew to Chicago from Albany to deliver his acceptance address before the convention. He was unable to walk even a short distance without canes and leg braces because of an attack of polio in 1921, and he wanted to silence the doubts about his health. "I pledge you," he told the delegates, "I pledge myself to a new deal for the American people." Thus, the Roosevelt program acquired a name before the electorate had the haziest notion of what the program might be.

ROOSEVELT | GARNER

I appreciate your willingness after these six arduous days to remain here, for I know well the sleepless hours which you and I have had. I regret that I am late, but I have no control over the winds of Heaven and could only be thankful for my Navy training.

The appearance before a National Convention of its nominee for President, to be formally notified of his selection, is unprecedented and unusual, but these are unprecedented and unusual times. I have started out on the tasks that lie ahead by breaking the absurd traditions that the candidate should remain in professed ignorance of what has happened for weeks until he is formally notified of that event many weeks later.

My friends, may this be the symbol of my intention to be honest and to avoid all hypocrisy or sham, to avoid all silly shutting of the eyes to the truth in this campaign. You have nominated me and I know it, and I am here to thank you for the honor.

Let it also be symbolic that in so doing I broke traditions. Let it be from now on the task of our Party to break foolish traditions. We will break foolish traditions and leave it to the Republican leadership, far more skilled in that art, to break promises.

Let us now and here highly resolve to resume the country's interrupted march along the path of real progress, of real justice, of real equality for all of our citizens, great and small. [. . .]

As we enter this new battle, let us keep always present with us some of the ideals of the party: The fact that the Democratic Party by tradition and by the continuing logic of history, past and present, is the bearer of liberalism and of progress and at the same time of safety to our institutions. And if this appeal fails, remember well, my friends, that a resentment against the failure of Republican leadership—and note well that in this campaign I shall not use the words "Republican Party," but I shall use, day in and day out, the words "Republican leadership"—the failure of Republican leaders to solve our trou:hles may degenerate into unreasoning radicalism. [. . .]

There are two ways of viewing the Government's duty in matters affecting economic and social life. The first sees to it that a favored few are helped and hopes that some of their prosperity will leak through, sift through, to labor, to the farmer, to the small business man. That theory belongs to the party of Toryism, and I had hoped that most of the Tories left this country in 1776.

But it is not and never will be the theory of the Democratic Party. This is no time for fear, for reaction, or for timidity. Here and now I invite those nominal Republicans who find that their conscience cannot be squared with the groping and the failure of their party leaders to join hands with us; here and now, in equal measure, I warn those nominal Democrats who squint at the future with their faces turned toward the past, and who feel no responsibility to the demands of the new time, that they are out of step with their Party.

Yes, the people of this country want a genuine choice this year, not a choice between two names for the same reactionary doctrine. Ours must be a party of liberal thought, of planned action, of enlightened international outlook, and of the greatest good to the greatest number of our citizens.

Now it is inevitable—and the choice is that of the times—it is inevitable that the main issue of this campaign should revolve about the clear fact of our economic condition, a depression so deep that it is without precedent in modern history. It will not do merely to state, as do Republican leaders to explain their broken promises of continued inaction, that the depression is worldwide. That was not their explanation of the apparent prosperity of 1928. The people will not forget the claim made by them then that prosperity was only a domestic product manufactured by a Republican President and a Republican Congress. If they claim paternity for the one they cannot deny paternity for the other. [. . .]

Never in history have the interests of all the people been so united in a single economic problem. Picture to yourself, for instance, the great groups of property owned by millions of our citizens, represented by credits issued in the form of bonds and mortgages—Government bonds of all kinds, Federal, State, county, municipal; bonds of industrial companies, of utility companies; mortgages on real estate in farms and cities, and finally the vast investments of the Nation in the railroads. What is the measure of the security of each of those groups? We know well that in our complicated, interrelated credit structure if any one of these credit groups collapses they may all collapse. Danger to one is danger to all.

How, I ask, has the present Administration in Washington treated the interrelationship of these credit groups? The answer is clear: It has not recognized that interrelationship existed at all. Why, the Nation asks, has Washington failed to understand that all of these groups, each and everyone, the top of the pyramid and the bottom of the pyramid, must be considered together, that each and every one of them is dependent on every other; each and every one of them affecting the whole financial fabric?

Statesmanship and vision, my friends, require relief to all at the same time. [. . .]

That is why we are going to make the voters understand that this is Nation is not merely a Nation of independence, but it is, if we are to surivive, bound to be a Nation of interdependence—town and city, and North and South, East and West. That is our goal, and that goal will be understood by the people of this country no matter where they live.

Cigar box with Roosevelt paper label.

There is an enormous amount of political and commemorative material associated with Franklin D. Roosevelt's presidency and his four presidential campaigns. Roosevelt and the New Deal, the name given to the president's domestic programs, became synonymous. While millions loved Roosevelt, others hated him with a passion unequaled in American political history.

(Above) Pressed-cardboard hangar, possibly intended as a lamp-chain pull.

(Right) Mirror with Roosevelt portrait.

Yes, when—not if—when we get the chance, the Federal Government will assume bold leadership in distress relief. For years Washington has alternated between putting its head in the sand and saying there is no large number of destitute people in our midst who need food and clothing, and then saying the States should take care of them, if they are. Instead of planning two and a half years ago to do what they are now trying to do, they kept putting it off from day to day, week to week, and month to month, until the conscience of America demanded action. [. . .]

Never before in modern history have the essential differences between the two major American parties stood out in such striking contrast as they do today. Republican leaders not only have failed in material things, they have failed in national vision, because in disaster they have held out no hope, they have pointed out no path for the people below to climb back to places of security and of safety in our American life. [. . .]

[I pledge you, I pledge myself, to a new deal for the American people.]

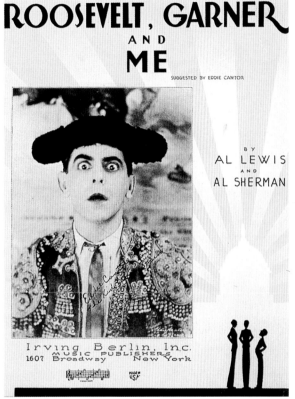

Sheet music, with a photograph of comedian Eddie Cantor, the "me" in the title.

Let us all here assembled constitute ourselves prophets of a new order of competence and of courage. This is more than a political campaign; it is a call to arms. Give me your help, not to win votes alone, but to win in this crusade to restore America to its own people.

Hoover Accepts the Nomination

The dispirited Republican Convention opened in Chicago on June 14, 1932. "There was not a single soul thus far I have met, stand-pat, Progressive or otherwise, who believes Hoover can be elected," Senator Hiram Johnson of California wrote. A few Republicans tried to start a movement to draft Calvin Coolidge, but the former president firmly ended such talk. Hoover was renominated on the first ballot. Speakers praised him as a leader who had saved the nation from communism and who "knows the burden of the heat of the day." The delegates paraded up and down the aisles for half an hour and balloons drifted down from the rafters. The convention adjourned after selecting Charles Curtis of Kansas for vice president. They left the task of saving the party from impending disaster in the president's hands.

In accepting the great honor you have brought me, I desire to speak so simply and so plainly that every man and woman in the United States who may hear or read my words cannot misunderstand.

The last three years have been a time of unparalleled economic calamity. They have been years of greater suffering and hardship than any which have come to the American people since the aftermath of the Civil War. [. . .]

If we look back over the disasters of these three years, we find that three quarters of the population of the globe has suffered from the flames of revolution. Many nations have been subject to constant change and vacillation of government. Others have resorted to dictatorship or tyranny in desperate attempts to preserve some sort of social order.

I may pause for one short illustration of the character of one single destructive force arising from these causes which we have been compelled to meet. That was its effect upon our financial structure. Foreign countries, in the face of their own failures not believing that we had the courage or ability to meet this crisis, withdrew from the United States over $2,400,000,000, including a billion in gold. Our own alarmed citizens withdrew over $1,600,000,000 of currency from our banks into hoarding. These actions, combined with the fears they generated, caused a shrinkage of credit available for conduct of industry and commerce by several times even these vast sums. Its visible expression was bank and business failures, demoralization of security and real property values, commodity prices, and employment. This was but one of the invading forces of destruction.

Two courses were open. We might have done nothing. That would have been utter ruin. Instead, we met the situation with proposals to private business and the Congress of the most gigantic program of economic defense and counter attack ever evolved in the history of the Republic. We put it into action.

Our measures have repelled these attacks of fear and panic. We have maintained the financial integrity of our Government. We have cooperated to restore and stabilize the situation abroad. As a nation we have paid every dollar demanded of us. We have used the credit of the Government to aid and protect our institutions, public and private. We have provided methods and assurances that there shall be none to suffer from hunger and cold. We have instituted measures to assist farmers and home owners. We have created vast

The 1932 presidential election came in the third year of the greatest economic depression ever experienced by the American people. The descent from the height of prosperity of the late 1920s had been rapid, bringing fear and uncertainty. During the 1920s, the United States was the most prosperous country in the world. American factories produced millions of automobiles, refrigerators, radios, phonographs, vacuum cleaners, and all sorts of manufactured goods. Wages were the highest in history.

In 1926, the president of the New York Stock Exchange declared that the average employee could become wealthy through stock investments. "The benefits of the capitalistic system are becoming practically universal," he boasted. Between 1923 and 1929, common stock prices rose about 200 percent. In his 1929 inaugural address, President Herbert Hoover had declared: "I have no fear for the future of our country. It is bright with hope." Less than eight months later, on October 29, 1929, stock prices at the New York Stock Exchange fell in the most disastrous day in the history of the market. This sharp downward plunge of the market triggered a terrible contraction in the economy. Stocks and bonds, ironically called securities, declined for the next three-and-a-half years.

There are many reasons for the economic collapse and the ensuing period known as the Great Depression. Democrats blamed it on Republican economic policies, such as the high protective tariff. Hoover and the Republicans argued that the European banking crises agencies for employment. Above all, we have maintained the sanctity of the principles upon which this Republic has grown great.

In a large sense the test of success of our program is simple. Our people, while suffering great hardships, have been and will be cared for. In the long view our institutions have been sustained intact and are now functioning with increasing confidence of the future. As a nation we are undefeated and unafraid. Government by the people has not been defiled.

of 1931 prevented the United States from coming out of the depression without serious hardships. He described the 17 months from October 1929 to April 1931 as "a period of a comparatively mild domestic readjustment such as the country had experienced before." The *Washington Post* which supported Hoover, denounced the Democrats for trying to make the economic situation a political issue. When "we give freedom to individuals and business," the newspaper editorialized, "we shouldn't blame the government if that freedom brings mistakes and depression and trouble." Former Democratic Senator James A. Reed of Missouri replied bitingly that as the Republican Party had maintained for 40 years that "it was the producer of prosperity, and now it says it has no control over financial and economic conditions, it has perpetrated a 40-year fraud upon the American people and has gained and kept office by false pretenses."

President Hoover attempted to use governmental power and prestige to check the deteriorating situation, but conditions worsened. Critics of Hoover claim that his policies moved too slowly and lacked imagination. His defenders maintain that, regardless of the president's efforts, the depression just had to run its course. But millions of Americans would not wait for the economic system to right itself. The depression had caused not only financial disaster but, perhaps more important, a loss in pride, status, and self-satisfaction. Prompt and immediate action was demanded. All indications pointed to a sweeping Democratic victory in the 1932 elections.

With the humility of one who by necessity has stood in the midst of this storm I can say with pride that the distinction for these accomplishments belongs not to the Government or to any individual. It is due to the intrepid soul of our people. It is to their character, their fortitude, their initiative, and their courage that we owe these results. We of this generation did not build the great Ship of State. But the policies I have inaugurated have protected and aided its navigation in this storm. These policies and programs have not been partisan. I gladly give tribute to those members of the Democratic Party in Congress whose patriotic cooperation against factional and demagogic opposition has assisted in a score of great undertakings. I likewise give credit to Democratic as well as Republican leaders among our citizens for their cooperation and help. [. . .]

I wish to say something of my conception of the relation of our Government to the people and of the responsibilities of both, particularly as applied to these times. The spirit and devising of this Government by the people was to sustain a dual purpose—on the one hand to protect our people among nations and in domestic emergencies by great national power, and on the other to preserve individual liberty and freedom through local government.

The function of the Federal Government in these times is to use its reserve powers and its strength for the protection of citizens and local governments by supporting our institutions against forces beyond their control. It is not the function of the Government to relieve individuals of their responsibilities to their neighbors, or to relieve private institutions of their responsibilities to the public, or of local government to the States, or of State governments to the Federal Government. In giving that protection and that aid the Federal Government must insist that all of them exert their responsibilities in full. It is vital that the programs of the Government shall not compete with or replace any of them but shall add to their initiative and their strength. It is vital that by the use of public revenues and public credit in emergency the Nation shall be strengthened and not weakened.

And in all these emergencies and crises, and in all our future policies, we must also preserve the fundamental principies of our social and economic system. That system is founded upon a conception of ordered freedom. The test of that freedom is that there should be maintained equality of opportunity to every individual so that he may achieve for himself the best to which his character, ability, and ambition entitle him. It is only by this release of initiative, this insistence upon individual responsibility, that we accrue the great sums of individual accomplishment which carry this Nation forward. This is not an individualism which permits men to run riot in selfishness or to override equality of opportunity for others. It permits no violation of ordered liberty. In the race after the false gods of materialism men and groups have forgotten their country. Equality of opportunity contains no conception of exploitation by any selfish, ruthless, class-minded men or groups. They have no place in the American system. As against these stand the guiding ideals and concepts of our Nation. I propose to maintain them.

The solution of our many problems which arise from the shifting scene of national life is not to be found in haphazard experimentation or by revolution. It must be through organic development of our national life under these ideals. It must secure that cooperative action which builds initiative and strength outside of government. It does not follow, because our difficulties are stupendous, because there are some souls timorous enough to doubt the validity and effectiveness of our ideals and our system, that we must turn to a State-controlled or State-directed social or economic system in order to cure our troubles. That is not liberalism; it is tyranny. It is the regimentation of men under autocratic bureaucracy with all its extinction of liberty, of hope, and opportunity. Of course, no man of understanding says that our system works perfectly. It does not. The human race is not perfect. Nevertheless, the movement of a true civilization is toward freedom rather than regimentation. This is our ideal.

Ofttimes the tendency of democracy in presence of national danger is to strike blindly, to listen to demagogues and slogans, all of which would destroy and would not save. We have refused to be stampeded into such courses. Ofttimes democracy elsewhere in the world has been unable to move fast enough to save itself in emergency. There have been disheartening delays and failures in legislation and private action which have added to the losses of our people, yet this democracy of ours has proved its ability to act.

Our emergency measures of the last three years form a definite strategy dominated in the background by these American principles and ideals, forming a continuous campaign waged against the forces of destruction on an ever widening or constantly shifting front.

Thus we have held that the Federal Government should in the presence of great national danger use its powers to give leadership to the initiative, the courage, and the fortitude of the people themselves; but it must insist upon individual, community, and state responsibility. [. . .]

My fellow citizens, the discussion of great problems of economic life and of government often seems abstract and cold. But within their right solution lie the happiness and hope of a great people. Without such solution all else is mere verbal sympathy.

Today millions of our fellow countrymen are out of work. Prices of the farmers' products are below a living standard. Many millions more who are in business or hold employment are haunted by fears for the future. No man with a spark of humanity can sit in my place without suffering from the picture of their anxieties and hardships before him day and night. They would be more than human if they were not led to blame their condition upon the government in power. I have understood their sufferings and have worked to the limits of my strength to produce action that would really help them.

Much remains to be done to attain recovery. The emergency measures now in action represent an unparalleled use of national power to relieve distress, to provide employment, to serve agriculture, to preserve the stability of the Government, to maintain the integrity of our institutions. Our policies prevent

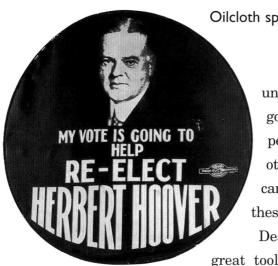

Oilcloth spare-tire cover for Hoover.

unemployment caused by floods of imported goods and laborers. Our policies preserve peace. They embrace cooperation with other nations in those fields in which we can serve. With patience and perseverance these measures will succeed.

Despite the dislocation of economic life our great tools of production and distribution are more efficient than ever before; our fabulous natural resources, our farms, our homes, our skill are unimpaired. From the hard-won experience of this depression we shall build stronger methods of prevention and stronger methods of protection to our people from the abuses which have become evident. We shall march to far greater accomplishment.

With united effort we can and will turn the tide toward the restoration of business, employment, and agriculture. It will call for the utmost devotion and wisdom. Every reserve of American courage and vision must be called upon to sustain us and to plan wisely for the future.

Through it all our first duty is to preserve unfettered that dominant American spirit which has produced our enterprise and individual character. That is the bedrock of the past, and that is the guaranty of the future. Not regimented mechanisms but free men is our goal. Herein is the fundamental issue. A representative democracy, progressive and unafraid to meet its problems, but meeting them upon the foundations of experience and not upon the wave of emotion or the insensate demands of a radicalism which grasps at every opportunity to exploit the sufferings of a people.

With these courses we shall emerge from this great national strain with our American system of life and government strengthened. Our people will be free to reassert their energy and enterprise in a society eager to reward in full measure those whose industry serves its well-being. Our youth will find the doors of equal opportunity still open.

The problems of the next few years are not only economic. They are also moral and spiritual. The present check to our material success must deeply stir our national conscience upon the purposes of life itself. It must cause us to revalue and reshape our drift from materialism to a higher note of individual and national ideals.

Underlying every purpose is the spiritual application of moral ideals which are the fundamental basis of happiness in a people. This is a land of homes, churches, schoolhouses dedicated to the sober and enduring satisfactions of family life and the rearing of children in an atmosphere of ideals and religious faith. Only with these high standards can we hold society together, and only from them can government survive or business prosper. They are the sole insurance to the safety of our children and the continuity of the Nation.

If it shall appear that while I have had the honor of the Presidency I have contributed the part required from this high office to bringing the Republic through this dark night, and if in my administration we shall see the break of dawn to a better day, I shall have done my part in the world. No man can have a greater honor than that.

I have but one desire: that is, to see my country again on the road to prosperity which shall be more sane and lasting through the lesson of experience, to see the principles and ideals of the American people perpetuated. [. . .]

★ Roosevelt's First ★ Inaugural Address

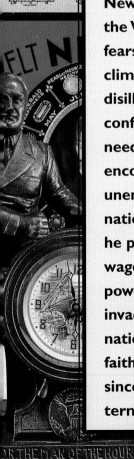

On Inaugural Day 1933, hunger marchers paraded in New York and Chicago as if in a ghastly mockery of the Washington ceremonies. It seemed that all the fears brought by the depression had come to a climax. Roosevelt's inaugural address gave hope to a disillusioned America. His assured tone and absolute confidence in the recovery of the country provided a needed tonic for a confused people. The president's encouraging voice urged immediate steps to end unemployment, to aid the farmer, and to bring about national recovery. If the Congress failed to respond, he promised to seek broad executive powers "to wage a war against the emergency, as great as the power that would be given to me if we were in fact invaded by a foreign foe." This vigorous assertion of national leadership inspired confidence and renewed faith in the democratic system of government. Not since George Washington had a president started his term of office with such popular support.

FRANKLIN D. ROOSEVELT

Franklin D. Roosevelt

I am certain that my fellow Americans expect that on my induction into the Presidency I will address them with a candor and a decision which the present situation of our Nation impels. This is preeminently the time to speak the truth, the whole truth, frankly and boldly. Nor need we shrink from honestly facing conditions in our country today. This great Nation will endure as it has endured, will revive and will prosper. So, first of all, let me assert my firm belief that the only thing we have to fear is fear itself—nameless, unreasoning, unjustified terror which paralyzes needed efforts to convert retreat into advance. In every dark hour of our national life a leadership of frankness and vigor has met with that understanding and support of the people themselves which is essential to victory. I am convinced that you will again give that support to leadership in these critical days.

In such a spirit on my part and on yours we face our common difficulties. They concern, thank God, only material things. Values have shrunken to fantastic levels; taxes have risen; our ability to pay has fallen; government of all kinds is faced by serious curtailment of income; the means of exchange are frozen in the currents of trade; the withered leaves of industrial enterprise lie on every side; farmers find no markets for their produce; the savings of many years in thousands of families are gone.

More important, a host of unemployed citizens face the grim problem of existence, and an equally great number toil with little return. Only a foolish optimist can deny the dark realities of the moment.

Yet our distress comes from no failure of substance. We are stricken by no plague of locusts. Compared with the perils which our forefathers conquered because they believed and were not afraid, we have still much to be thankful for. Nature still offers her bounty and human efforts have multiplied it. Plenty is at our doorstep, but a generous use of it languishes in the very sight of the supply. Primarily this is because the rulers of the

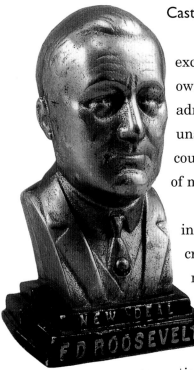

Castiron bank of Roosevelt.

exchange of mankind's goods have failed, through their own stubbornness and their own incompetence, have admitted their failure, and abdicated. Practices of the unscrupulous money changers stand indicted in the court of public opinion, rejected by the hearts and minds of men.

True they have tried, but their efforts have been cast in the pattern of an outworn tradition. Faced by failure of credit they have proposed only the lending of more money. Stripped of the lure of profit by which to induce our people to follow their false leadership, they have resorted to exhortations, pleading tearfully for restored confidence. They know only the rules of a generation of self-seekers. They have no vision, and when there is no vision the people perish.

The money changers have fled from their high seats in the temple of our civilization. We may now restore that temple to the ancient truths. The measure of the restoration lies in the extent to which we apply social values more noble than mere monetary profit.

Happiness lies not in the mere possession of money; it lies in the joy of achievement, in the thrill of creative effort. The joy and moral stimulation of work no longer must be forgotten in the mad chase of evanescent profits. These dark days will be worth all they cost us if they teach us that our true destiny is not to be ministered unto but to minister to ourselves and to our fellow men.

Recognition of the falsity of material wealth as the standard of success goes hand in hand with the abandonment of the false belief that public office and high political position are to be valued only by the standards of pride of place and personal profit; and there must be an end to a conduct in banking and in business which too often has given to a sacred trust the likeness of callous and selfish wrongdoing. Small wonder that confidence languishes, for it thrives only on honesty, on honor, on the sacredness of obligations, on faithful protection, on unselfish performance; without them it cannot live.

Restoration calls, however, not for changes in ethics alone. This Nation asks for action, and action now.

Our greatest primary task is to put people to work. This is no unsolvable problem if we face it wisely and courageously. It can be accomplished in part by direct recruiting by the Government itself, treating the task as we would treat the emergency of a war, but at the same time, through this employment, accomplishing greatly needed projects to stimulate and reorganize the use of our natural resources.

Hand in hand with this we must frankly recognize the overbalance of population in our industrial centers and, by engaging on a national scale in a redistribution, endeavor to provide a better use of the land for those best fitted for the land. The task can be helped by definite efforts to raise the values of agricultural products and with this the power to purchase the output of our cities. It can be helped by preventing realistically the tragedy of the growing loss through foreclosure of our small homes and our farms. It can be helped by insistence that the Federal, State, and local governments act forthwith on the demand that their cost be drastically reduced. It can be helped by the unifying of relief activities which today are often scattered, uneconomical, and unequal. It can be helped by national planning for and supervision

In 1933 the District of Columbia began issuing a limited number of license plates for each presidential inauguration.

of all forms of transportation and of communications and other utilities which have a definitely public character. There are many ways in which it can be helped, but it can never be helped merely by talking about it. We must act and act quickly.

Finally, in our progress toward a resumption of work we require two safeguards against a return of the evils of the old order; there must be a strict supervision of all banking and credits and investments; there must be an end to speculation with other people's money, and there must be provision for an adequate but sound currency.

There are the lines of attack. I shall presently urge upon a new Congress in special session detailed measures for their fulfillment[. . . .]

The basic thought that guides these specific means of national recovery is not narrowly nationalistic. It is the insistence, as a first consideration, upon the interdependence of the various elements in all parts of the United States—a recognition of the old and permanently important manifestation of the American spirit of the pioneer. It is the way to recovery. It is the immediate way. It is the strongest assurance that the recovery will endure. [. . .]

If I read the temper of our people correctly, we now realize as we have never realized before our interdependence on each other; that we can not merely take but we must give as well; that if we are to go forward, we must move as a trained and loyal army willing to sacrifice for the good of a common discipline, because without such discipline no progress is made, no leadership becomes effective. We are, I know, ready and willing to submit our lives and property to such discipline, because it makes possible a leadership which aims at a larger good. This I propose to offer, pledging that the larger purposes will bind upon us all as a sacred obligation with a unity of duty hitherto evoked only in time of armed strife.

With this pledge taken, I assume unhesitatingly the leadership of this great army of our people dedicated to a disciplined attack upon our common problems.

Action in this image and to this end is feasible under the form of government

Tin automobile license attachments. The Democratic Party favored repeal of the Prohibition Amendment. This occurred with the ratification of the Twenty-first Amendment (December 1933).

which we have inherited from our ancestors. Our Constitution is so simple and practical that it is possible always to meet extraordinary needs by changes in emphasis and arrangement without loss of essential form. That is why our constitutional system has proved itself the most superbly enduring political mechanism the modern world has produced. It has met every stress of vast expansion of territory, of foreign wars, of bitter internal strife, of world relations.

It is to be hoped that the normal balance of executive and legislative authority may be wholly adequate to meet the unprecedented task before us. But it may be that an unprecedented demand and need for undelayed action may call for temporary departure from that normal balance of public procedure.

I am prepared under my constitutional duty to recommend the measures

The peak period for political neckties was from the 1930s through the 1960s.

that a stricken nation in the midst of a stricken world may require. These measures, or such other measures as the Congress may build out of its experience and wisdom, I shall seek, within my constitutional authority, to bring to speedy adoption.

But in the event that the Congress shall fail to take one of these two courses, and in the event that the national emergency is still critical, I shall not evade the clear course of duty that will then confront me. I shall ask the Congress for the one remaining instrument to meet the crisis—broad Executive power to wage a war against the emergency, as great as the power that would be given to me if we were in fact invaded by a foreign foe.

For the trust reposed in me I will return the courage and the devotion that befit the time. I can do no less.

We face the arduous days that lie before us in the warm courage of the national unity; with the clear consciousness of seeking old and precious moral values; with the clean satisfaction that comes from the stern performance of duty by old and young alike. We aim at the assurance of a rounded and permanent national life.

We do not distrust the future of essential democracy. The people of the United States have not failed. In their need they have registered a mandate that they want direct, vigorous action. They have asked for discipline and direction under leadership. They have made me the present instrument of their wishes. In the spirit of the gift I take it.

In this dedication of a Nation we humbly ask the blessing of God. May He protect each and every one of us. May He guide me in the days to come.

Second "Fireside Chat," May 7, 1933

The president's optimism and self-assurance were conveyed in a series of very successful radio addresses which came to be known as "the fireside chats." There were about 30 such broadcasts during his 12 years in office. "My friends," he would begin, and then, in simple but eloquent language, he would explain a new program or policy. Eleanor Roosevelt later wrote that, after her husband's death, people would stop her in the street to say, "He used to talk to me about my government." After the first fireside chat, a few days after he took office, Roosevelt asked the public to share their views with him. The White House received thousands of letters from ordinary people who were convinced that the president was willing to listen to them. And he did.

ANKLIN D. ROOSEVE

anklin D. Rooseve

OR THE MAN OF THE HOUR

ROOSEVELT   GARNER

On a Sunday night a week after my Inauguration I used the radio to tell you about the banking crisis and the measures we were taking to meet it. [. . .] Tonight, eight weeks later, I come for the second time to give you my report—in the same spirit and by the same means to tell you about what we have been doing and what we are planning to do.

Two months ago we were facing serious problems. The country was dying by inches. It was dying because trade and commerce had declined to dangerously low levels; prices for basic commodities were such as to destroy the value of the assets of national institutions such as banks, savings banks, insurance companies, and others. These institutions, because of their great needs, were foreclosing mortgages, calling loans, refusing credit. Thus there was actually in process of destruction the property of millions of people who had borrowed money on that property in terms of dollars which had had an entirely different value from the level of March, 1933. That situation in that crisis did not call for any complicated consideration of economic panaceas or fancy plans. We were faced by a condition and not a theory.

There were just two alternatives: The first was to allow the foreclosures to continue, credit to be withheld, and money to go into hiding, and thus forcing liquidation and bankruptcy of banks, railroads, and insurance companies and a recapitalizing of all business and all property on a lower level. This alternative meant a continuation of what is loosely called "deflation," the net result of which would have been extraordinary hardship on all property owners and, incidentally, extraordinary hardships on all persons working for wages through an increase in unemployment and a further reduction of the wage scale.

It is easy to see that the result of this course would have not only economic effects of a very serious nature but social results that might bring incalculable harm. Even before I was inaugurated I came to the conclusion that such a policy was too much to ask the American people to bear. It involved not only a further loss of homes, farms, savings, and wages but also a loss of spiritual values—the loss of that sense of security for the present and the future so necessary to the peace and contentment of the individual and of his family. When you destroy these things you will find it difficult to establish confidence of any sort in the future.

It was clear that mere appeals from Washington for confidence and the mere lending of more money to shaky institutions could not stop this downward course. A prompt program applied as quickly as possible seemed to me not only justified but imperative to our national security. The Congress, and when I say Congress I mean the members of both political parties, fully understood this and gave me generous and intelligent support. The members of Congress realized that the methods of normal times had to be replaced in the emergency by measures which were suited to the serious and pressing requirements of the moment. There was no actual surrender of power, Congress still retained its constitutional authority and no one has the slightest desire to change the balance of these powers. The function of Congress is to decide what has to be done and to select the appropriate agency to carry out its will. This policy it has strictly adhered to. The only thing that has been happening has been to designate the President as the agency to carry out certain of the purposes of the Congress. This was constitutional and in keeping with the past American tradition.

The legislation which has been passed or in the process of enactment can properly be considered as part of a well-grounded plan.

First, we are giving opportunity of employment to one-quarter of a million of the unemployed, especially the young men who have dependents, to go into the forestry and flood prevention work. This is a big task because it means feeding, clothing, and caring for nearly twice as many men as we have in the regular army itself. In creating this civilian conservation corps we are killing two birds with one stone. We are clearly enhancing the value of our natural resources and second, we are relieving an appreciable amount of actual distress. This great group of men have entered upon their work on a purely voluntary basis, no military training is involved and we are conserving not only our natural resources but our human resources. One of the great values to this work is the fact that it is direct and requires the intervention of very little machinery.

Second, I have requested the Congress and have secured action upon a proposal to put the great properties owned by our Government at Muscle Shoals to work after long years of wasteful inaction, and with this a broad plan for the improvement of a vast area in the Tennessee Valley. It will add to the comfort and happiness of hundreds of thousands of people and the incident benefits will reach the entire nation.

Next, the Congress is about to pass legislation that will greatly ease the mortgage distress among the farmers and the home owners of the nation, by providing for the easing of the burden of debt now bearing so heavily upon millions of our people.

Our next step in seeking immediate relief is a grant of half a billion dollars to help the states, counties, and municipalities in their duty to care for those who need direct and immediate relief.

The Congress also passed legislation authorizing the sale of beer in such states as desired. This has already resulted in considerable reemployment and, incidentally, has provided much needed tax revenue.

We are planning to ask the Congress for legislation to enable the Government to undertake public works, thus stimulating directly and indirectly the employment of many others in well-considered projects.

Further legislation has been taken up which goes much more fundamentally into our economic problems. The Farm Relief Bill seeks by the use of several methods, alone or together, to bring about an increased return to farmers for their major farm products, seeking at the same time to prevent in the days to come disastrous over-production which so often in the past has kept farm commodity prices far below a reasonable return. This measure provides wide powers for emergencies. The extent of its use will depend entirely upon what the future has in store.

Well-considered and conservative measures will likewise be proposed which will attempt to give to the industrial workers of the country a more fair wage return, prevent cut-throat competition and unduly long hours for labor, and at the same time to encourage each industry to prevent over-production.

Our Railroad Bill falls into the same class because it seeks to provide and make certain definite planning by the railroads themselves, with the assistance of the Government, to eliminate the duplication and waste that is now resulting in railroad receiverships and continuing operating deficits. I am certain that the people of this country understand and approve the broad purposes behind these new governmental policies relating to agriculture and industry and transportation. We found ourselves faced with more agricultural products than we could possibly consume ourselves and surpluses which other nations did not have the cash to buy from us except at prices ruinously low. We have found our factories able to turn out more goods than we could possibly consume, and at the same time we were faced with a falling export demand. We found ourselves with more facilities to transport goods and crops than there were goods and crops to be transported. All of this has been caused in large part by a complete lack of planning and a complete failure to understand the danger signals that have been flying ever since the close of the World War. The people of this country have been erroneously encouraged to believe that they could keep on increasing the output of farm and factory indefinitely and that some magician would find ways and means for that increased output to be consumed with reasonable profit to the producer.

Today we have reason to believe that things are a little better than they were two months ago. Industry has picked up, railroads are carrying more freight, farm prices are better, but I am not going to indulge in issuing proclamations of overenthusiastic assurance. We cannot bally-ho ourselves back to

Sheet music, circa 1934. Marching with the slogan, "We Do Our Part," many National Recovery Administration (NRA) parades were held in American cities to encourage participation in the program.

More important legislation was passed during Franklin D. Roosevelt's first term than in any other four years in U. S. history. Roosevelt and his advisers believed that immediate federal action was needed to restore confidence in the economic system. Their goal was to maintain capitalism but, at the same time, to reform— not destroy—the

economic system that had brought hardships to so many. The main point of the NRA was to ration the nation's business among the surviving corporations. It never really worked—and it was declared unconstitutional by a unanimous Supreme Court in 1935.

prosperity. I am going to be honest at all times with the people of the country. I do not want the people of this country to take the foolish course of letting this improvement come back on another speculative wave. I do not want the people to believe that because of unjustified optimism we can resume the ruinous practice of increasing our crop output and our factory output in the hope that a kind providence will find buyers at high prices. Such a course may bring us immediate and false prosperity but it will be the kind of prosperity that will lead us into another tailspin. It is wholly wrong to call the measure that we have taken Government control of farming, control of industry, and

Cardboard pencil box with simulated wood-carved motif, a relic of the 1932 presidential election.

A bewildering number of laws were passed under the New Deal, and dozens of agencies were created to meet the problems of relief, recovery, and reform. Although these policies did not completely alleviate depression

conditions, they did return hope to the United States. Unemployment was reduced and the government's vast relief programs cared for millions still without work. Farm prices rose dramatically. In 1936, corn sold at $1.26 a bushel compared to 24 cents in 1933. The price of wheat reached $1.51 a bushel; it had been 47 cents four years earlier. Weekly factory wages increased an estimated 65 percent. The New Deal programs quickly made Roosevelt the hero of the working class.

control of transportation. It is rather a partnership between Government and farming and industry and transportation, not partnership in profits, for the profits would still go to the citizens, but rather a partnership in planning and partnership to see that the plans are carried out. [. . .]

We are working toward a definite goal, which is to prevent the return of conditions which came very close to destroying what we call modern civilization. The actual accomplishment of our purpose cannot be attained in a day. Our policies are wholly within purposes for which our American Constitutional Government was established 150 years ago.

I know that the people of this country will understand this and will also understand the spirit in which we are undertaking this policy. I do not deny that we may make mistakes of procedure as we carry out the policy. I have no expectation of making a hit every time I come to bat. What I seek is the highest possible batting average, not only for myself but for the team. Theodore Roosevelt once said to me: "If I can be right 75 percent of the time I shall come up to the fullest measure of my hopes."

Much has been said of late about Federal finances and inflation, the gold standard, etc. Let me make the facts very simple and my policy very clear. In the first place, government credit and government currency are really one and the same thing. Behind government bonds there is only a promise to pay. Behind government currency we have, in addition to the promise to pay, a reserve of gold and a small reserve of silver. In this connection it is worth while remembering that in the past the government has agreed to redeem nearly thirty billions of its debts and its currency in gold, and private corporations in this country have agreed to redeem another sixty or seventy billions of securities and mortgages in gold. The government and private corporations were making these agreements when they knew full well that all of the gold in the United States amounted to only between three and four billions and that all of the gold in all of the world amounted to only about eleven billions.

If the holders of these promises to pay started in to demand gold the first comers would get gold for a few days and they would amount to about one twenty-fifth of the holders of the securities and the currency. The other twenty-four people out of twenty-five, who did not happen to be at the top of the line, would be told politely that there was no more gold left. We have decided to treat all twenty-five in the same way in the interest of justice and the exercise of the constitutional powers of this government. We have placed every one on the same basis in order that the general good may be preserved.

Nevertheless, gold, and to a partial extent silver, are perfectly good bases for currency and that is why I decided not to let any of the gold now in the country go out of it.

A series of conditions arose three weeks ago which very readily might have meant, first, a drain on our gold by foreign countries, and secondly, as a result of that, a flight of American capital, in the form of gold, out of our country. It is not exaggerating the possibility to tell you that such an occurrence might well have taken from us the major part of our gold reserve and resulted in such a further weakening of our government and private credit as to bring on actual panic conditions and the complete stoppage of the wheels of industry.

The Administration has the definite objective of raising commodity prices to such an extent that those who have borrowed money will, on the average, be able to repay that money in the same kind of dollar which they borrowed. We do not seek to let them get such a cheap dollar that they will be able to pay back a great deal less than they borrowed. In other words, we seek to correct a wrong and not to create another wrong in the opposite direction. That is why powers are being given to the Administration to provide, if necessary, for an enlargement of credit, in order to correct the existing wrong. These powers will be used when, as, and if it may be necessary to accomplish the purpose.

Hand in hand with the domestic situation which, of course, is our first concern, is the world situation, and I want to emphasize to you that the domestic situation is inevitably and deeply tied in with the conditions in all of the other nations of the world. In other words, we can get, in all probability, a fair measure of prosperity return in the United States, but it will not be permanent unless we get a return to prosperity all over the world.

In the conferences which we have held and are holding with the leaders of other nations, we are seeking four great objectives. First, a general reduction of armaments and through this the removal of the fear of invasion and armed attack, and, at the same time, a reduction in armament costs, in order to help in the balancing of government budgets and the reduction of taxation. Secondly, a cutting down of the trade barriers, in order to re-start the flow of exchange of crops and goods between nations. Third, the setting up of a stabilization of currencies, in order that trade can make contracts ahead. Fourth, the reestablishment of friendly relations and greater confidence between all nations.

Our foreign visitors these past three weeks have responded to these

Roosevelt's birthday received national attention during his presidency. Parties were held throughout the country raising money to aid crippled children. This charity event was the forerunner of the March of Dimes. Poster is by Howard Chandler Christy.

AMERICA "TO OUR PRESIDENT"

JOIN THE
President's Birthday Party
HELP THE CRIPPLED CHILDREN

Get Your Membership Card Here
25¢ upward

purposes in a very helpful way. All of the Nations have suffered alike in this great depression. They have all reached the conclusion that each can best be helped by the common action of all. It is in this spirit that our visitors have met with us and discussed our common problems. The international conference that lies before us must succeed. The future of the world demands it and we have each of us pledged ourselves to the best joint efforts to this end.

To you, the people of this country, all of us, the members of the Congress and the members of this Administration owe a profound debt of gratitude. Throughout the depression you have been patient. You have granted us wide powers, you have encouraged us with a wide-spread approval of our purposes. Every ounce of strength and every resource at our command we have devoted to the end of justifying your confidence. We are encouraged to believe that a wise and sensible beginning has been made. In the present spirit of mutual confidence and mutual encouragement we go forward.

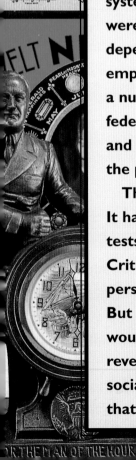

Social Security

The Social Security Act of 1935 created a national system of old-age insurance in which most employees were compelled to participate. The legislation depended upon moneys raised by taxing both employers and employees to create a fund to support a number of social programs—pensions for the aged, federal-state programs for unemployment insurance, and provisions for dependent poor children and for the physically handicapped.

The 1935 Act was a landmark in American history. It has been amended many times but has withstood tests in the courts and changes of political mood. Critics cited the traditional American reliance on personal responsibility and decried the entire idea. But Roosevelt correctly assumed that Social Security would grow in scope and coverage over time. It reversed historic assumptions about the nature of social responsibility, and it established the proposition that the individual had clear-cut social rights.

ANKLIN D. ROOSEVE

anklin D. Rooseve

OR THE MAN OF THE HOUR

ROOSEVELT   GARNER

In addressing you on June 8, 1934, I summarized the main objectives of our American program. Among these was, and is, the security of the men, women, and children of the Nation against certain hazards and vicissitudes of life. This purpose is an essential part of our task. In my annual message to you I promised to submit a definite program of action. This I do in the form of a report to me by a Committee on Economic Security, appointed by me for the purpose of surveying the field and of recommending the basis of legislation.

I am gratified with the work of this Committee and of those who have helped it: The Technical Board on Economic Security drawn from various departments of the Government, the Advisory Council on Economic Security, consisting of informed and public-spirited private citizens and a number of other advisory groups, including a committee on actuarial consultants, a medical advisory board, a dental advisory committee, a hospital advisory committee, a public-health advisory committee, a child-welfare committee and an advisory committee on employment relief. All of those who participated in this notable task of planning this major legislative proposal are ready and willing, at any time, to consult with and assist in any way the appropriate Congressional committees and members, with respect to detailed aspects.

It is my best judgment that this legislation should be brought forward with a minimum of delay. Federal action is necessary to, and conditioned upon, the action of States. Forty-four legislatures are meeting or will meet soon. In order that the necessary State action may be taken promptly it is important that the Federal Government proceed speedily.

The detailed report of the Committee sets forth a series of proposals that will appeal to the sound sense of the American people. It has not attempted the impossible, nor has it failed to exercise sound caution and consideration of all of the factors concerned: the national credit, the rights

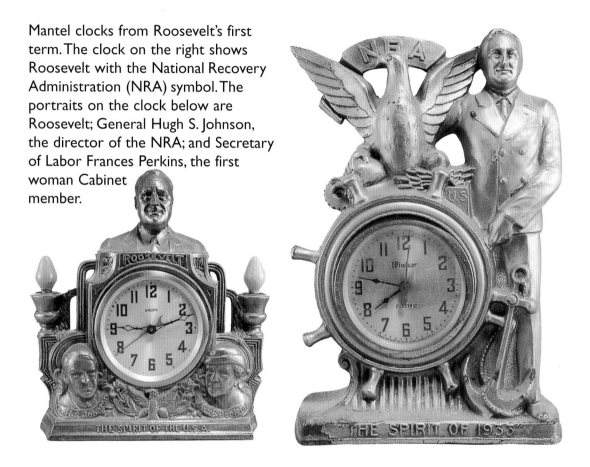

Mantel clocks from Roosevelt's first term. The clock on the right shows Roosevelt with the National Recovery Administration (NRA) symbol. The portraits on the clock below are Roosevelt; General Hugh S. Johnson, the director of the NRA; and Secretary of Labor Frances Perkins, the first woman Cabinet member.

and responsibilities of States, the capacity of industry to assume financial responsibilities and the fundamental necessity of proceeding in a manner that will merit the enthusiastic support of citizens of all sorts.

It is overwhelmingly important to avoid any danger of permanently discrediting the sound and necessary policy of Federal legislation for economic security by attempting to apply it on too ambitious a scale before actual experience has provided guidance for the permanently safe direction of such efforts. The place of such a fundamental in our future civilization is too precious to be jeopardized now by extravagant action. It is a sound idea—a sound ideal. Most of the other advanced countries of the world have already adopted it and their experience affords the knowledge that social insurance can be made a sound and workable project.

Three principles should be observed in legislation on this subject. First, the system adopted, except for the money necessary to initiate it, should be self-sustaining in the sense that funds for the payment of insurance benefits should not come from the proceeds of general taxation. Second, excepting in old-age insurance, actual management should be left to the States subject to standards established by the Federal Government. Third, sound financial management of the funds and the reserves, and protection of the credit structure of the Nation should be assured by retaining Federal control over all funds through trustees in the Treasury of the United States.

At this time, I recommend the following types of legislation looking to economic security:

1. Unemployment compensation.

2. Old-age benefits, including compulsory and voluntary annuities.

3. Federal aid to dependent children through grants to States for the support of existing mothers' pension systems and for services for the protection and care of homeless, neglected, dependent, and crippled children.

4. Additional Federal aid to State and local public-health agencies and the strengthening of the Federal Public Health Service. I am not at this time recommending the adoption of so-called "health insurance," although groups representing the medical profession are cooperating with the Federal Government in the further study of the subject and definite progress is being made.

With respect to unemployment compensation, I have concluded that the most practical proposal is the levy of a uniform Federal payroll tax, 90 percent of which should be allowed as an offset to employers contributing under a compulsory State unemployment compensation act. The purpose of this is to afford a requirement of a reasonably uniform character for all States cooperating with the Federal Government and to promote and encourage the passage of unemployment compensation laws in the States. The 10 percent not thus offset should be used to cover the costs of Federal and State administration of this broad system. Thus, States will largely administer unemployment compensation, assisted and guided by the Federal Government. An unemployment compensation system should be constructed in such a way as to afford every practicable aid and incentive toward the larger purpose of employment stabilization. This can be helped by the intelligent planning of both public and private employment. It also can be helped by correlating the system with public employment so that a person who has exhausted his benefits may be eligible for some form of public work as is recommended in this report. Moreover, in order to encourage the stabilization of private employment, Federal legislation should not foreclose the States from establishing means for inducing industries to afford an even greater stabilization of employment.

In the important field of security for our old people, it seems necessary to adopt three principles: First, noncontributory old-age pensions for those who are now too old to build up their own insurance. It is, of course, clear that for perhaps 30 years to come funds will have to be provided by the States and the Federal Government to meet these pensions. Second, compulsory contributory annuities which in time will establish a self-supporting system for those now young and for future generations.

Items from the 1932–34 period. (Left) A tin automobile license attachment from Roosevelt's 1932 campaign. (Opposite) British-made etched glass crystal goblet commemorating Roosevelt's first inauguration and the repeal of Prohibition. This is perhaps the finest modern glass item with a political theme.

Third, voluntary contributory annuities by which individual initiative can increase the annual amounts received in old age. It is proposed that the Federal Government assume one-half of the cost of the old-age pension plan, which ought ultimately to be supplanted by self-supporting annuity plans.

The amount necessary at this time for the initiation of unemployment compensation, old-age security, children's aid, and the promotion of public health, as outlined in the report of the Committee on Economic Security, is approximately $100,000,000.

The establishment of sound means toward a greater future economic security of the American people is dictated by a prudent consideration of the hazards involved in our national life. No one can guarantee this country against the dangers of future depressions but we can reduce these dangers. We can eliminate many of the factors that cause economic depressions, and we can provide the means of mitigating their results. This plan for economic security is at once a measure of prevention and a method of alleviation.

We pay now for the dreadful consequence of economic insecurity—and dearly. This plan presents a more equitable and infinitely less expensive means of meeting these costs. We cannot afford to neglect the plain duty before us. I strongly recommend action to attain the objectives sought in this report.

Putting People to Work

ANKLIN D. ROOSEVE

anklin D. Rooseve

In 1935, most relief programs—that is, programs to help the unemployed—had been combined under a new agency, the Works Progress Administration (WPA). The WPA attempted to make use of an individual's skill, whether it be sewing or translating books into Braille. At its peak in November 1938, nearly 3.3 million persons were on is payroll. When the WPA ended in 1941, it had provided work for a total of 8 million people. Among its 250,000 projects, the WPA built or improved more than 2,500 hospitals, 5,900 school buildings, 1,000 airports, and nearly 13,000 playgrounds. The WPA also gave employment to artists, musicians, actors, singers, and writers. Critics called these make-work programs a "boondoggle"—a waste of money. However, they put people back to work. Their salaries, besides giving them the ability to buy things, also helped to stimulate the depressed economy. Roosevelt discussed the work program in this "fireside chat."

ROOSEVELT   GARDEN

Since my annual message to the Congress on January fourth, last, I have not addressed the general public over the air. In the many weeks since that time the Congress has devoted itself to the arduous task of formulating legislation necessary to the country's welfare. It has made and is making distinct progress.

Before I come to any of the specific measures, however, I want to leave in your minds one clear fact. The Administration and the Congress are not proceeding in any haphazard fashion in this task of government. Each of our steps has a definite relationship to every other step. The job of creating a program for the Nation's welfare is, in some respects, like the building of a ship. At different points on the coast where I often visit they build great seagoing ships, and when one of these ships is under construction and the steel frames have been set in the keel, it is difficult for a person who does not know ships to tell how it will finally look when it is sailing the high seas. It may seem confused to some, but out of the multitude of detailed parts that go into the making of the structure the creation of a useful instrument for man ultimately comes.

It is that way with the making of a national policy. [. . .]

My most immediate concern is in carrying out the purposes of the great work program just enacted by the Congress. Its first objective is to put men and women now on the relief rolls to work and, incidentally, to assist materially in our already unmistakable march toward recovery. I shall not confuse my discussion by a multitude of figures. So many figures are quoted to prove so many things. Sometimes it depends upon what paper you read and what broadcast you hear. Therefore, let us keep our minds on two or three simple, essential facts in connection with this problem of unemployment. It is true that while business and industry are definitely better our relief rolls are still too large. However, for the first time in five years the relief rolls have declined instead of increased during the winter months. They are still declining. The simple fact is that many million more people have private work today than two years ago today or one year ago today, and every day that passes offers more chances to work for those who want to work. In spite of the fact that unemployment remains a serious problem here as in every other nation, we have come to recognize the possibility and the necessity of certain helpful remedial measures. These measures are of two kinds. The first is to make provisions intended to relieve, to minimize, and to prevent future unemployment; the second is to establish the practical means to help those who are unemployed in this present emergency. Our social security legislation is an attempt to answer the first of these questions; our work relief program the second.

The program for social security now pending before the Congress is a necessary part of the future unemployment policy of the government. While our present and projected expenditures for work relief are wholly within the reasonable limits of our national credit resources, it is obvious that we cannot continue to create governmental deficits for that purpose year after year. We must begin now to make provision for the future. That is why our social security program is an important part of the complete picture. It proposes, by means of old age pensions, to help those who have reached the age of retirement to give up their jobs and thus give to the younger generation greater opportunities for work and to give to all a feeling of security as they look toward old age.

The unemployment insurance part of the legislation will not only help to guard the individual in future periods of lay-off against dependence upon relief, but it will, by sustaining purchasing power, cushion the shock of economic distress. Another helpful feature of unemployment insurance is the incentive it will give to employers to plan more carefully in order that unemployment may be prevented by the stabilizing of employment itself.

Provisions for social security, however, are protections for the future. Our responsibility for the immediate necessities of the unemployed has been met by the Congress through the most comprehensive work plan in the history of the Nation. Our problem is to put to work three-and-one-half million employable persons now on the relief rolls. It is a problem quite as much for private industry as for the government.

We are losing no time getting the government's vast work relief program underway, and we have every reason to believe that it should be in full swing by autumn. In directing it, I shall recognize six fundamental principles:

First, the projects should be useful.

Secondly, the projects should be of a nature that a considerable proportion of the money spent will go into wages for labor.

Sheet music, an excellent example of Art Deco design.

Third, projects which promise ultimate return to the Federal Treasury of a considerable proportion of the costs will be sought.

Fourth, funds allotted for each project should be actually and promptly spent and not held over until later years.

Fifth, in all cases projects must be of a character to give employment to those on the relief rolls.

And finally, projects will be allocated to localities or relief areas in relation to the number of workers on relief rolls in those areas.

Next, I think that it will interest you to know exactly how we shall direct

Metal donkey carrying a beer barrel and pictures of Roosevelt and Garner.

the work as a federal government.

First I have set up a Division of Applications and Information to which all proposals for the expenditure of money must go for preliminary study and consideration.

Secondly, after this Division of Applications and Information has sifted those projects, they will be sent to an Allotment Division composed of representatives of the more important governmental agencies charged with carrying on work relief projects. The group will also include representatives of cities, and of labor, farming, banking, and industry. This Allotment Division will consider all of the recommendations submitted to it and such projects as they approve will be next submitted to the President who under the Act is required to make final allocations.

The next step will be to notify the proper government agency in whose field the project falls, and also to notify another agency which I am creating— a Progress Division. This Division will have the duty of coordinating the purchases of materials and supplies and of making certain that people who are employed will be taken from the relief rolls. It will also have the responsibility of determining work payments in various localities, of making full use of existing employment services and to assist people engaged in relief work to move as rapidly as possible back into private employment when such employment is available. Moreover, this Division will be charged with keeping projects moving on schedule.

Finally, I have felt it to be essentially wise and prudent to avoid, so far as possible, the creation of new governmental machinery for supervising this work. The National Government now has at least sixty different agencies with the staff and the experience and the competence necessary to carry on the two hundred and fifty or three hundred kinds of work that will be undertaken. These agencies, therefore, will simply be doing on a somewhat enlarged scale the same sort of things that they have been doing. This will make certain that the largest possible portion of the funds allotted will be spent for actually creating new work and not for building up expensive overhead organizations here in Washington.

For many months preparations have been under way. The allotment of funds for desirable projects has already begun. The key men for the major responsibilities of this great task already have been selected. I well realize that the country is expecting before this year is out to see the "dirt fly," as they say, in carrying on the work, and I assure my fellow citizens that no energy will be spared in using these funds effectively to make a major attack upon the problem of unemployment.

Our responsibility is to all of the people in this country. This is a great national crusade to destroy enforced idleness which is an enemy of the human spirit generated by this depression. Our attack upon these enemies must be without stint and without discrimination. No sectional, no political distinctions can be permitted.

It must, however, be recognized that when an enterprise of this character is extended over more than three thousand counties throughout the Nation, there may be occasional instances of inefficiency, bad management, or misuse of funds. When cases of this kind occur, there will be those, of course, who will try to tell you that the exceptional failure is characteristic of the entire endeavor. It should be remembered that in every big job there are some imperfections. There are chiselers in every walk of life; there are those in every industry who are guilty of unfair practices, every profession has its black sheep, but long experience in government has taught me that the exceptional instances of wrong-doing in government are probably less numerous than in almost every other line of endeavor. The most effective means of preventing such evils in this work relief program will be the eternal vigilance of the American people themselves. I call upon my fellow citizens everywhere to cooperate with me in making this the most efficient and the cleanest example of public enterprise the world has ever seen.

It is time to provide a smashing answer for those cynical men who say that a democracy cannot be honest and efficient. If you will help, this can be done. I, therefore, hope you will watch the work in every corner of this Nation. Feel free to criticize. Tell me of instances where work can be done better, or where improper practices prevail. Neither you nor I want criticism conceived in a purely fault-finding or partisan spirit, but I am jealous of the right of every citizen to call to the attention of his or her government examples of how the public money can be more effectively spent for the benefit of the American people.

I now come, my friends, to a part of the remaining business before the Congress. It has under consideration many measures which provide for the rounding out of the program of economic and social reconstruction with which we have been concerned for two years. I can mention only a few of them tonight, but I do not want my mention of specific measures to be interpreted as lack of interest in or disapproval of many other important proposals that are pending.

The National Industrial Recovery Act expires on the sixteenth of June. After careful consideration, I have asked the Congress to extend the life of this useful agency of government. As we have proceeded with the administration

Roosevelt mantle clock picturing the president ("Man of the Hour") at the helm of a ship. From 1913 to 1920 Roosevelt had served as assistant secretary of the Navy; he often used the language of ships and the sea in his speeches, as in the second paragraph of this address.

of this Act, we have found from time to time more and more useful ways of promoting its purposes. No reasonable person wants to abandon our present gains—we must continue to protect children, to enforce minimum wages, to prevent excessive hours, to safeguard, define and enforce collective bargaining, and, while retaining fair competition, to eliminate so far as humanly possible, the kinds of unfair practices by selfish minorities which unfortunately did more than anything else to bring about the recent collapse of industries.

There is likewise pending before the Congress legislation to provide for the elimination of unnecessary holding companies in the public utility field.

I consider this legislation a positive recovery measure. Power production in this country is virtually back to the 1929 peak. The operating companies in the gas and electric utility field are by and large in good condition. But under holding company domination the utility industry has long been hopelessly at war within itself and with public sentiment. By far the greater part of the general decline in utility securities had occurred before I was inaugurated. The absentee management of unnecessary holding company control has lost touch with and has lost the sympathy of the communities it pretends to serve.

Even more significantly, it has given the country as a whole an uneasy apprehension of overconcentrated economic power.

You and I know that a business that loses the confidence of its customers and the good will of the public cannot long continue to be a good risk for the investor. This legislation will serve the investor by ending the conditions which have caused that lack of confidence and good will. It will put the public utility operating industry on a sound basis for the future, both in its public relations and in its internal relations.

This legislation will not only in the long run result in providing lower electric and gas rates to the consumer, but it will protect the actual value and earning power of properties now owned by thousands of investors who have little protection under the old laws against what used to be called frenzied finance. It will not destroy values.

Not only business recovery, but the general economic recovery of the Nation will be greatly stimulated by the enactment of legislation designed to improve the status of our transportation agencies. There is need for legislation providing for the regulation of interstate transportation by buses and trucks, to regulate transportation by water, new provisions for strengthening our Merchant Marine and air transport, measures for the strengthening of the Interstate Commerce Commission to enable it to carry out a rounded conception of the national transportation system in which the benefits of private ownership are retained, while the public stake in these important services is protected by the public's government.

And finally, the reestablishment of public confidence in the banks of the Nation is one of the most hopeful results of our efforts as a Nation to reestablish public confidence in private banking. We all know that private banking actually exists by virtue of the permission of and regulation by the people as a whole, speaking through their government. Wise public policy, however, requires not only that banking be safe but that its resources be most fully utilized, in the economic life of the country. To this end it was decided more than twenty years ago that the government should assume the responsibility of providing a means by which the credit of the Nation might be controlled, not by a few private banking institutions, but by a body with public prestige and authority. The answer to this demand was the Federal Reserve System. Twenty years of experience with this system have justified the efforts made to create it, but these twenty years have shown by experience definite possibilities for improvement. Certain proposals made to amend the Federal Reserve Act deserve prompt and favorable action by the Congress. They are a minimum of wise readjustment of our Federal Reserve system in the light of past experience and present needs.

These measures I have mentioned are, in large part, the program which under my constitutional duty I have recommended to the Congress. They are essential factors in a rounded program for national recovery. They contemplate the enrichment of our national life by a sound and rational ordering of its various elements and wise provisions for the protection of the weak against the strong.

Never since my inauguration in March, 1933, have I felt so unmistakably the atmosphere of recovery. But it is more than the recovery of the material basis of our individual lives. It is the recovery of confidence in our democratic processes and institutions. We have survived all of the arduous burdens and the threatening dangers of a great economic calamity. We have in the darkest moments of our national trials retained our faith in our own ability to master our destiny. Fear is vanishing and confidence is growing on every side, renewed faith in the vast possibilities of human beings to improve their material and spiritual status through the instrumentality of the democratic form of government. That faith is receiving its just reward. For that we can be thankful to the God who watches over America.

Thanks in large part to his economic policies, which were very popular, Roosevelt won reelection in 1936 in a landslide over Republican candidate Alf Landon, governor of Kansas. FDR received 60.8 percent of the popular vote and 523 of 531 electoral votes—the most one-sided election victory in American history.

Items pictured from the 1936 campaign include (bottom left) an assortment of Roosevelt buttons (including one issued by the Young Democrats of Kansas, which mimics the sunflower motif used in Landon campaign items); (bottom right) felt novelties with plastic button inserts of Landon and Roosevelt; (opposite top and left) Roosevelt tin automobile attachments. The plate at the top is a rebus item [Rose+velt]; (opposite bottom) Graphic poster in the WPA art style distributed by the New York State American Labor Party. Herbert Lehman was governor of New York and running for reelection.

★ Supreme Court Reorganization ★

Emboldened by his landslide re-election in 1936, Franklin Roosevelt soon committed the worst political blunder of his political career. With his power and prestige soaring, the president moved against the most formidable opponent of New Deal legislation, the Supreme Court of the United States. During Roosevelt's first term, the Court's majority had adopted a narrow interpretation regarding the federal government's powers. Already, nine major New Deal initiatives had been declared unconstitutional. The real problem, Roosevelt came to feel, lay not with the Constitution but with the Court. Since so many decisions had been handed down by a divided bench, any reform should be aimed at swelling the Court majority. Yet, the president moved cautiously because he knew Court packing violated taboos. He sought a formula that both had historical precedent, and which would divert attention from his desire for a more liberal Court by raising a new issue of judicial reform.

On February 5, 1937, Roosevelt sent Congress his plan for reorganizing the judiciary. The president had neither mentioned this issue during the recent campaign or had he discussed it with congressional leaders.

I have recently called the attention of the Congress to the dear need for a comprehensive program to reorganize the administrative machinery of the Executive Branch of our Government. I now make a similar recommendation to the Congress in regard to the Judicial Branch of the Government, in order that it also may function in accord with modern necessities.

The Constitution provides that the President "shall from time to time give to the Congress information of the State of the Union, and recommend to their consideration such measures as he shall judge necessary and expedient." No one else is given a similar mandate. It is therefore the duty of the President to advise the Congress in regard to the Judiciary whenever he deems such information or recommendation necessary.

I address you for the further reason that the Constitution vests in the Congress direct responsibility in the creation of courts and judicial offices and in the formulation of rules of practice and procedure. It is, therefore, one of the definite duties of the Congress constantly to maintain the effective functioning of the Federal Judiciary.

The Judiciary has often found itself handicapped by insufficient personnel with which to meet a growing and more complex business. It is true that the physical facilities of conducting the business of the courts have been greatly improved, in recent years, through the erection of suitable quarters, the provision of adequate libraries, and the addition of subordinate court officers. But in many ways these are merely the trappings of judicial office. They play a minor part in the processes of justice.

Since the earliest days of the Republic, the problem of the personnel of the courts has needed the attention of the Congress. For example, from the beginning, over repeated protest to President Washington, the Justices of the Supreme Court were required to "ride Circuit" and, as Circuit Justices, to hold trials throughout the length and breadth of the land—a practice which endured over a century.

In almost every decade since 1789, changes have been made by the Congress whereby the numbers of judges and the duties of Judges in federal courts have been altered in one way or another. The Supreme Court was established with six members in 1789; it was reduced to five in 1801; it was increased to seven in 1807; it was increased to nine in 1837; it was increased to ten in 1863; it was reduced to seven in 1866; it was increased to nine in 1869.

The simple fact is that today a new need for legislative action arises because the personnel of the Federal Judiciary is insufficient to meet the business before them. A growing body of our citizens complain of the complexities, the delays, and the expense of litigation in United States Courts.

A letter from the Attorney General, which I submit herewith justifies by reasoning and statistics the common impression created by our overcrowded federal dockets—and it proves the need for additional judges.

Delay in any court results in injustice.

It makes lawsuits a luxury available only to the few who can afford them or who have property interests to protect which are sufficiently large to repay the cost. Poorer litigants are compelled to abandon valuable rights or to accept inadequate or unjust settlements because of sheer inability to finance or to await the end of a long litigation. Only by speeding up the processes of the law and thereby reducing their cost, can we eradicate the growing impression that the courts are chiefly a haven for the well-to-do.

Delays in the determination of appeals have the same effect. Moreover, if trials of original actions are expedited and existing accumulations of cases are reduced, the volume of work imposed on the Circuit Courts of Appeals will further increase.

The attainment of speedier justice in the courts below will enlarge the task of the Supreme Court itself. And still more work would be added by the recommendation which I make later in this message for the quicker determination of constitutional questions by the highest court.

Even at the present time the Supreme Court is laboring under a heavy burden. Its difficulties in this respect were superficially lightened some years ago by authorizing the court, in its discretion, to refuse to hear appeals in many classes of cases. This discretion was so freely exercised that in the last fiscal year, although 867 petitions for review were presented to the Supreme Court, it declined to hear 717 cases. If petitions in behalf of the Government are excluded, it appears that the court permitted private litigants to prosecute appeals in only 108 cases out of 803 applications. Many of the refusals were doubtless warranted. But can it be said that full justice is achieved when a court is forced by the sheer necessity of keeping up with its business to decline, without even an explanation, to hear 87 percent of the cases presented to it by private litigants?

It seems clear, therefore, that the necessity of relieving present congestion extends to the enlargement of the capacity of all the federal courts.

Apart of the problem of obtaining a sufficient number of judges to dispose of cases is the capacity of the judges themselves. This brings forward the question of aged or infirm judges—a subject of delicacy and yet one which requires frank discussion.

In the federal courts there are in all 237 life tenure permanent judgeships. Twenty-five of them are now held by judges over seventy years of age and eligible to leave the bench on full pay. Originally no pension or retirement allowance was provided by the Congress. When after eighty years of our national history the Congress made provision for pensions, it found a well-entrenched tradition among judges to cling to their posts, in many instances far beyond their years of physical or mental capacity. Their salaries were small. As with other men, responsibilities and obligations accumulated. No alternative had been open to them except to attempt to perform the duties of their offices to the very edge of the grave.

In exceptional cases, of course, judges, like other men, retain to an advanced age full mental and physical vigor. Those not so fortunate are often unable to perceive their own infirmities. "They seem to be tenacious of the appearance of adequacy." The voluntary retirement law of 1869 provided, therefore, only a partial solution. That law, still in force, has not proved effective in inducing aged judges to retire on a pension.

This result had been foreseen in the debates when the measure was being considered. It was then proposed that when a judge refused to retire upon reaching the age of seventy, an additional judge should be appointed to assist in the work of the court. The proposal passed the House but was eliminated in the Senate.

With the opening of the twentieth century, and the great increase of population and commerce, and the growth of a more complex type of litigation, similar proposals were introduced in the Congress. To meet the situation, in 1913, 1914, 1915 and 1916, the Attorneys General then in office recommended to the Congress that when a district or a circuit judge failed to retire at the age of seventy, an additional judge be appointed in order that the affairs of the court might be promptly and adequately discharged.

In 1919 a law was finally passed providing that the President "may" appoint additional district and circuit judges, but only upon a finding that the incumbent judge over seventy "is unable to discharge efficiently all the duties of his office by reason of mental or physical disability of permanent character." The discretionary and indefinite nature of this legislation has rendered it ineffective. No President should be asked to determine the ability or disability of any particular judge.

The duty of a judge involves more than presiding or listening to testimony or arguments. It is well to remember that the mass of details involved in the average of law cases today is vastly greater and more complicated than even twenty years ago. Records and briefs muse be read; statutes, decisions, and extensive material of a technical, scientific, statistical and economic nature must be searched and studied; opinions must be formulated and written. The modern tasks of judges call for the use of full energies.

Modern complexities call also for a constant infusion of new blood in the courts, just as it is needed in executive functions of the Government and in private business. A lowered mental or physical vigor leads men to avoid an examination of complicated and changed conditions. Little by little, new facts become blurred through old glasses fitted, as it were, for the needs of another generation, older men, assuming that the scene is the same as it was in the past, cease to explore or inquire into the present or the future.

We have recognized this truth in the civil service of the nation and of many states by compelling retirement on pay at the age of seventy. We have recognized it in the Army and Navy by retiring officers at the age of sixty-four. A number of states have recognized it by providing in their constitutions for compulsory retirement of aged judges.

Life tenure of judges, assured by the Constitution, was designed to place the courts beyond temptations or influences which might impair their judgments: it was not intended to create a static judiciary. A constant and systematic addition of younger blood will vitalize the courts and better equip them to recognize and apply the essential concepts of justice in the light of the needs and the facts of an ever-changing world.

It is obvious, therefore, from both reason and experience, that some provision must be adopted, which will operate automatically to supplement the work of older judges and accelerate the work of the court.

We therefore, earnestly recommend that the necessity of an increase in the number of judges be supplied by legislation providing for the appointment of additional judges in all federal courts, without exception, where there are incumbent judges of retirement age who do not choose to retire or to resign. If an elder judge is not in fact incapacitated, only good can come from the presence of an additional judge in the crowded state of the dockets; if the capacity of an elder judge is in fact impaired, the appointment of an additional judge is indispensable. This seems to be a truth which cannot be contradicted.

I also recommend that the Congress provide machinery for taking care of sudden or long-standing congestion in the lower courts. The Supreme Court should be given power to appoint an administrative assistant who may be called a Proctor. He would be charged with the duty of watching the calendars and the business of all the courts in the federal system. The Chief Justice thereupon should be authorized to make a temporary assignment of any circuit or district judge hereafter appointed in order that he may serve as long as needed in any circuit or district where the courts are in arrears.

I attach a carefully considered draft of a proposed bill, which if enacted, would, I am confident, afford substantial relief. The proposed measure also contains a limit on the total number of judges who might thus be appointed and also a limit on the potential size of any one of our federal courts.

These proposals do not raise any issue of constitutional law. They do not suggest any form of compulsory retirement for incumbent judges. Indeed, those who have reached the retirement age, but desire to continue their judicial work, would be able to do so under less physical and mental strain and would be able to play a useful part in relieving the growing congestion in the business of our courts. Among them are men of eminence and great ability whose services the Government would be loath to lose. If, on the other hand, any judge eligible for retirement should feel that his court would suffer because of an increase in its membership, he may retire or resign under already existing provisions of law if he wishes so to do. In this connection let me say that the pending proposal to extend to the Justices of the Supreme Court the same retirement privileges now available to other federal judges, has my entire approval.

One further matter requires immediate attention. We have witnessed the spectacle of conflicting decisions in both trial and appellate courts on the constitutionality of every form of important legislation. Such a welter of uncomposed differences of judicial opinion has brought the law, the courts, and, indeed, the entire administration of justice dangerously near to disrepute.

A federal statute is held legal by one judge in one district; it is simultaneously held illegal by another judge in another district. An act valid in one judicial circuit is invalid in another judicial circuit. Thus rights fully accorded to one group of citizens may be denied to others. As a practical matter this means that for periods running as long as one year or two years or three years—until final determination can be made by the Supreme Court—the law loses its most indispensable element—equality.

Moreover, during the long processes of preliminary motions, original trials, petitions for rehearings, appeals, reversals on technical grounds requiring re-trials, motions before the Supreme Court, and the final hearing by the highest tribunal—during all this time labor, industry, agriculture, commerce, and the Government itself go through an unconscionable period of uncertainty and embarrassment. And it is well to remember that during these long processes the normal operations of society and government are handicapped in many cases by differing and divided opinions in the lower courts and by the lack of any clear guide for the dispatch of business. Thereby our legal system is fast losing another essential of justice—certainty.

Finally, we find the processes of government itself brought to a complete stop from time to time by injunctions issued almost automatically, sometimes even without notice to the Government, and not infrequently in clear violation of the principle of equity that injunctions should be granted only in those rare cases of manifest illegality and irreparable damage against which the ordinary course of the law offers no protection. Statutes which the Congress enacts are set aside or suspended for long periods of time, even in cases to which the Government is not a party.

In the uncertain state of the law, it is not difficult for the ingenuous to devise novel reasons for attacking the validity of new legislation or its application. While these questions are laboriously brought to issue and debated through a series of courts, the Government must stand aside. It matters not that the Congress has enacted the law, that the Executive has signed it and that the administrative machinery is waiting to function. Government by injunction lays a heavy hand upon normal processes; and no important statute can take effect—against any individual or organization with the means to employ lawyers and engage in wide-flung litigation—until it has passed through the whole hierarchy of the courts. Thus the judiciary, by postponing the effective date of Acts of the Congress, is assuming an additional function and is coming more and more to constitute a scattered, loosely organized, and slowly operating third house of the National Legislature.

This state of affairs has come upon the nation gradually over a period of decades. In my annual message to this Congress I expressed some views and some hopes.

Now, as an immediate step, I recommend that the Congress provide that no decision, injunction, judgment, or decree on any constitutional question be promulgated by any federal court without previous and ample notice to the Attorney General and an opportunity for the United States to present evidence and be heard. This is to prevent court action on the constitutionality of Acts of the Congress in suits between private individuals, where the Government is not a party to the suit, without giving opportunity to the Government of the United States to defend the law of the land.

I also earnestly recommend that in cases in which any court of first instance determines a question of constitutionality, the Congress provide that there shall be a direct and immediate appeal to the Supreme Court, and that such cases take precedence over all other matters pending in that court. Such legislation will, I am convinced, go far to alleviate the inequality, uncertainty, and delay in the disposition of vital questions of constitutionality arising under our fundamental law.

My desire is to strengthen the administration of justice and to make it a more effective servant of public need. In the American ideal of government the courts find an essential and constitutional place. In striving to fulfill that ideal, not only the judges but the Congress and the Executive as well, must do all in their power to bring the judicial organization and personnel to the high standards of usefulness which sound and efficient government and modern conditions require.

This message has dealt with four present needs:

First, to eliminate congestion of calendars and to make the judiciary as a whole less static by the constant and systematic addition of new blood to its personnel; second, to make the judiciary more elastic by providing for temporary transfers of circuit and district judges to those places where federal courts are most in arrears; third, to furnish the Supreme Court practical assistance in supervising the conduct of business in the lower courts; fourth, to eliminate inequality, uncertainty, and delay now existing in the determination of constitutional questions involving federal statutes.

If we increase the personnel of the federal courts so that cases may be promptly decided in the first instance, and may be given adequate and prompt hearing on all appeals; if we invigorate all the courts by the persistent infusion of new blood; if we grant to the Supreme Court further power and responsibility in maintaining the efficiency of the entire federal judiciary; and if we assure government participation in the speedier consideration and final determination of all constitutional questions, we shall go a long way toward our high objectives. If these measures achieve their aim, we may be relieved of the necessity of considering any fundamental changes in the powers of the courts or the constitution of our Government—changes which involve consequences so far-reaching as to cause uncertainty as to the wisdom of such course.

The "Four Freedoms" Speech

In November 1940, Roosevelt was elected to a third term, easily defeating his rival, Wendell Willkie, and breaking the two-term precedent established by George Washington. On January 6, 1941, Roosevelt delivered his State of the Union message to a joint session of Congress. In it, he proposed an ambitious "lend-lease" program, in which the United States would remain neutral but would provide "ships, planes, tanks, [and] guns" to democracies to help in the fight against totalitarianism. In the speech, Roosevelt also outlined the four "essential human freedoms" as a body of humane wartime objectives. Denying that his vision was utopian, Roosevelt proclaimed it attainable in "our own time and generation." It comprised one more chapter, he said, in the country's quest for a world order in which free countries would work together in creating a friendly, civilized society. By the end of 1941, the U.S. was involved in the Second World War.

I address you, the Members of the Seventy-seventh Congress, at a moment unprecedented in the history of the Union. I use the word "unprecedented," because at no previous time has American security been as seriously threatened from without as it is today.

Since the permanent formation of our Government under the Constitution, in 1789, most of the periods of crisis in our history have related to our domestic affairs. Fortunately, only one of these—the four-year War Between the States—ever threatened our national unity. Today, thank God, one hundred and thirty million Americans, in forty-eight States, have forgotten points of the compass in our national unity.

It is true that prior to 1914 the United States often had been disturbed by events in other Continents. We had even engaged in two wars with European nations and in a number of undeclared wars in the West Indies, in the Mediterranean and in the Pacific for the maintenance of American rights and for the principles of peaceful commerce. But in no case had a serious threat been raised against our national safety or our continued independence.

What I seek to convey is the historic truth that the United States as a nation has at all times maintained clear, definite opposition to any attempt to lock us in behind an ancient Chinese wall while the procession of civilization went past. Today, thinking of our children and of their children, we oppose enforced isolation for ourselves or for any other part of the Americas. [. . .]

Every realist knows that the democratic way of life is at this moment being directly assailed in every part of the world—assailed either by arms, or by secret spreading of poisonous propaganda by those who seek to destroy unity and promote discord in nations that are still at peace.

During sixteen long months this assault has blotted out the whole pattern of democratic life in an appalling number of independent nations,

No president had ever won (or sought) a third term until Franklin Roosevelt in 1940. Though his margin of victory was not as great as in 1936, Roosevelt easily defeated his Republican challenger, Wendell Willkie. FDR received 54.8 percent of the popular vote and 449 electoral votes to 44.8 percent and 82 electoral votes for Willkie.

(Right) Silk bandannas for Willkie and Roosevelt using statements made by each candidate. The Willkie item contains a challenge to the president to "debate the fundamental issues of the campaign."
(Bottom) Inaugural program, 1941.

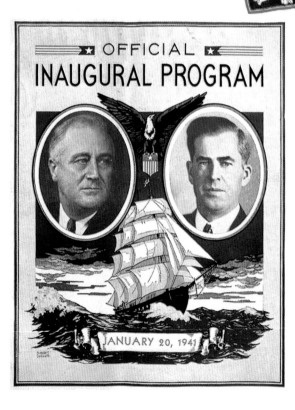

Tin face powder compacts shown both open and closed.

great and small. The assailants are still on the march, threatening other nations, great and small.

Therefore, as your President, performing my constitutional duty to "give to the Congress information of the state of the Union," I find it, unhappily, necessary to report that the future and the safety of our country and of our democracy are overwhelmingly involved in events far beyond our borders.

Armed defense of democratic existence is now being gallantly waged in four continents. If that defense fails, all the population and all the resources of Europe, Asia, Africa, and Australasia will be dominated by the conquerors. Let us remember that the total of those populations and their resources in those four continents greatly exceeds the sum total of the population and the resources of the whole of the Western Hemisphere—many times over.

In times like these it is immature—and incidentally, untrue—for anybody to brag that an unprepared America, single-handed, and with one hand tied behind its back, can hold off the whole world.

No realistic American can expect from a dictator's peace international generosity, or return of true independence, or world disarmament, or freedom of expression, or freedom of religion—or even good business.

Such a peace would bring no security for us or for our neighbors. "Those, who would give up essential liberty to purchase a little temporary safety, deserve neither liberty nor safety." [. . .]

The need of the moment is that our actions and our policy should be devoted primarily—almost exclusively—to meeting this foreign peril. For all our domestic problems are now a part of the great emergency. [. . .]

Our national policy is this:

First, by an impressive expression of the public will and without regard to partisanship, we are committed to all-inclusive national defense.

Second, by an impressive expression of the public will and without regard to partisanship, we are committed to full support of all those resolute peoples, everywhere, who are resisting aggression and are thereby keeping war away from our Hemisphere. By this support, we express our determination that the democratic cause shall prevail; and we strengthen the defense and the security of our own nation.

Third, by an impressive expression of the public will and without regard to partisanship, we are committed to the proposition that principles of morality and considerations for our own security will never permit us to acquiesce in a peace dictated by aggressors and sponsored by appeasers. We know that enduring peace cannot be bought at the cost of other people's freedom. [. . .]

To change a whole nation from a basis of peacetime production of implements of peace to a basis of wartime production of implements of war is no small task. And the greatest difficulty comes at the beginning of the program, when new tools, new plant facilities, new assembly lines, and new ship ways must first be constructed before the actual materiel begins to flow steadily and speedily from them. [. . .]

New circumstances are constantly begetting new needs for our safety. I shall ask this Congress for greatly increased new appropriations and authorizations to carry on what we have begun.

I also ask this Congress for authority and for funds sufficient to manufacture additional munitions and war supplies of many kinds, to be turned over to those nations which are now in actual war with aggressor nations. [. . .]

Let us say to the democracies: "We Americans are vitally concerned in your defense of freedom. We are putting forth our energies, our resources, and our organizing powers to give you the strength to regain and maintain a free world. We shall send you, in ever-increasing numbers, ships, planes, tanks, guns. This is our purpose and our pledge." [. . .]

In the future days, which we seek to make secure, we look forward to a world founded upon four essential human freedoms.

The first is freedom of speech and expression—everywhere in the world.

The second is freedom of every person to worship God in his own way— everywhere in the world.

The third is freedom from want—which, translated into world terms, means economic understandings which will secure to every nation a healthy peacetime life for its inhabitants—everywhere in the world.

The fourth is freedom from fear—which, translated into world terms, means a world-wide reduction of armaments to such a point and in such a thorough fashion that no nation will be in a position to commit an act of physical aggression against any neighbor—anywhere in the world.

That is no vision of a distant millennium. It is a definite basis for a kind of world attainable in our own time and generation. That kind of world is the very antithesis of the so-called new order of tyranny which the dictators seek to create with the crash of a bomb.

To that new order we oppose the greater conception—the moral order. A good society is able to face schemes of world domination and foreign revolutions alike without fear.

Since the beginning of our American history, we have been engaged in change—in a perpetual peaceful revolution—a revolution which goes on steadily, quietly adjusting itself to changing conditions—without the concentration camp or the quick-lime in the ditch. The world order which we seek is the cooperation of free countries, working together in a friendly, civilized society.

This nation has placed its destiny in the hands and heads and hearts of its millions of free men and women; and its faith in freedom under the guidance of God. Freedom means the supremacy of human rights everywhere. Our support goes to those who struggle to gain those rights or keep them. Our strength is our unity of purpose.

To that high concept there can be no end save victory.

Message on the Pearl Harbor Attack

On Sunday morning, December 7, 1941, Japanese naval aircrafts bombed America's Pearl Harbor naval base in Hawaii. The attack was a complete surprise. While events had been indicating the possibility of confrontation with Japan for some time, this sudden attack stunned the nation.

The day after the Pearl Harbor attack, President Roosevelt asked Congress to accept the "state of war" that Japan's "unprovoked and dastardly attack" had thrust upon the United States. Three days later, Germany and Italy declared war on the United States. Congress again accepted the challenge. The United States now confronted war on both the Atlantic and the Pacific.

Yesterday, December 7, 1941—a date which will live in infamy—the United States of America was suddenly and deliberately attacked by naval and air forces of the Empire of Japan.

The United States was at peace with that nation and, at the solicitation of Japan, was still in conversation with the government and its emperor looking toward the maintenance of peace in the Pacific.

Indeed, one hour after Japanese air squadrons had commenced bombing in Oahu, the Japanese ambassador to the United States and his colleagues delivered to the Secretary of State a formal reply to a recent American message. While this reply stated that it seemed useless to continue the existing diplomatic negotiations, it contained no threat or hint of war or armed attack.

It will be recorded that the distance of Hawaii from Japan makes it obvious that the attack was deliberately planned many days or even weeks ago. During the intervening time, the Japanese government has deliberately sought to deceive the United States by false statements and expressions of hope for continued peace.

The attack yesterday on the Hawaiian islands has caused severe damage to American naval and military forces. Very many American lives have been lost. In addition, American ships have been reported torpedoed on the high seas between San Francisco and Honolulu.

Yesterday, the Japanese government also launched an attack against Malaya.

Last night, Japanese forces attacked Hong Kong.

Last night, Japanese forces attacked Guam.

Last night, Japanese forces attacked the Philippine Islands.

Last night, the Japanese attacked Wake Island.

This morning, the Japanese attacked Midway Island.

Japan has, therefore, undertaken a surprise offensive extending

1942 calendar with the patriotic slogan "Remember Pearl Harbor."

throughout the Pacific area. The facts of yesterday speak for themselves. The people of the United States have already formed their opinions and well understand the implications to the very life and safety of our nation.

As commander in chief of the Army and Navy, I have directed that all measures be taken for our defense.

Always will we remember the character of the onslaught against us.

No matter how long it may take us to overcome this premeditated invasion, the American people in their righteous might will win through to absolute victory.

I believe I interpret the will of the Congress and of the people when I assert that we will not only defend ourselves to the uttermost, but will make very certain that this form of treachery shall never endanger us again.

Hostilities exist. There is no blinking at the fact that our people, our territory and our interests are in grave danger.

With confidence in our armed forces—with the unbounding determination of our people—we will gain the inevitable triumph—so help us God.

I ask that the Congress declare that since the unprovoked and dastardly attack by Japan on Sunday, December 7, a state of war has existed between the United States and the Japanese empire.

Creamware plate with
Roosevelt transfer portrait.

Throughout the 1930s, the United States clung to an isolationist policy, believing that even if war should come abroad, the nation would be able to remain neutral. The bitter memories of the First World War (1914–18) and the dread of a future one, helped to create a public opinion that earnestly searched for peace. But, European events, climaxed by the German invasion of Poland in September 1939, indicated to many Americans that their own interests were more deeply involved in foreign events than they had realized. "The nation will remain a neutral nation, but I cannot ask that every American remain neutral in thought as well.... Even a neutral cannot be asked to close his mind or conscience." After this statement by the president, Congress repealed the ban on sale of munitions to foreign nations (November 1939). Neutrality was rapidly discarded as the United States, led by a president determined to aid the European democracies, edged closer toward war.

The Yalta Agreement

As the Second World War ended, the leaders of the United States, Great Britain, and the Soviet Union—Roosevelt, Winston Churchill, and Joseph Stalin—met at Yalta in February 1945. There, the "Big Three" discussed the postwar fate of Germany (which would be occupied by the three powers plus France), Japan, Poland, Yugoslavia, and other countries. They also agreed to create a world organization—the United Nations.

In photos taken at the Yalta Conference, Roosevelt appeared sick and exhausted. Less than two months later, on April 12, 1945, Franklin D. Roosevelt died of a massive cerebral hemorrhage.

I. WORLD ORGANIZATION

It was decided:

1. That a United Nations conference on the proposed world organization should be summoned for Wednesday, 25 April, 1945, and should be held in the United States of America.

2. The nations to be invited to this conference should be:

   (a) the United Nations as they existed on 8 February, 1945; and

   (b) Such of the Associated Nations as have declared war on the common enemy by 1 March, 1945. (For this purpose, by the term "Associated Nations" was meant the eight Associated Nations and Turkey.) When the conference on world organization is held, the delegates of the United Kingdom and United State of America will support a proposal to admit to original membership two Soviet Socialist Republics, i.e., the Ukraine and White Russia. [. . .]

II. DECLARATION OF LIBERATED EUROPE

The following declaration has been approved:

The Premier of the Union of Soviet Socialist Republics, the Prime Minister of the United Kingdom, and the President of the United States of America have consulted with each other in the common interests of the people of their countries and those of liberated Europe. They jointly declare their mutual agreement to concert during the temporary period of instability in liberated Europe the policies of their three Governments in assisting the peoples liberated from the domination of Nazi Germany and the peoples of the former Axis satellite states of Europe to solve by democratic means their pressing political and economic problems.

The establishment of order in Europe and the rebuilding of national economic life must be achieved by processes which will enable the liberated peoples to destroy the last vestiges of nazism and fascism and to create democratic institutions of their own choice. This is a principle of the Atlantic Charter—the right of all people to choose the form of government under which they will live—the restoration of sovereign rights and self-government to those peoples who have been forcibly deprived to them by the aggressor nations.

To foster the conditions in which the liberated people may exercise these rights, the three governments will jointly assist the people in any European liberated state or former Axis state in Europe where, in their judgment conditions require,

(a) to establish conditions of internal peace;

(b) to carry out emergency relief measures for the relief of distressed peoples;

(c) to form interim governmental authorities broadly representative of all democratic elements in the population and pledged to the earliest possible establishment through free elections of Governments responsive to the will of the people; and

(d) to facilitate where necessary the holding of such elections.

The three Governments will consult the other United Nations and provisional authorities or other Governments in Europe when matters of direct interest to them are under consideration.

When, in the opinion of the three Governments, conditions in any European liberated state or former Axis satellite in Europe make such action necessary, they will immediately consult together on the measure necessary to discharge the joint responsibilities set forth in this declaration.

By this declaration we reaffirm our faith in the principles of the Atlantic Charter, our pledge in the Declaration by the United Nations and our determination to build in cooperation with other peace-loving nations world order, under law, dedicated to peace, security, freedom, and general well-being of all mankind.

In issuing this declaration, the three powers express the hope that the Provisional Government of the French Republic may be associated with them in the procedure suggested.

III. DISMEMBERMENT OF GERMANY

It was agreed that Article 12 (a) of the Surrender terms for Germany should be amended to read as follows:

"The United Kingdom, the United States of America, and the Union of Soviet Socialist Republics shall possess supreme authority with respect to Germany. In the exercise of such authority they will take such steps, including the complete dismemberment of Germany as they deem requisite for future peace and security."

The study of the procedure of the dismemberment of Germany was referred to a committee consisting of Mr. Anthony Eden, Mr. John Winant, and Mr. Fedor T. Gusev. This body would consider the desirability of associating with it a French representative.

IV. ZONE OF OCCUPATION FOR THE FRENCH AND CONTROL COUNCIL FOR GERMANY.

It was agreed that a zone in Germany, to be occupied by the French forces, should be allocated France. This zone would be formed out of the British and American zones and its extent would be settled by the British and Americans in consultation with the French Provisional Government.

It was also agreed that the French Provisional Government should be invited to become a member of the Allied Control Council for Germany.

V. REPARATION

The following protocol has been approved:

On the Talks Between the Heads of Three Governments at the Crimean Conference on the Question of the German Reparations in Kind:

1. Germany must pay in kind for the losses caused by her to the Allied nations in the course of the war. Reparations are to be received in the first instance by those countries which have borne the main burden of the war, have suffered the heaviest losses, and have organized victory over the enemy.

2. Reparation in kind is to be exacted from Germany in three following forms:

(a) Removals within two years from the surrender of Germany or the cessation of organized resistance from the national wealth of Germany located on the territory of Germany herself as well as outside her territory (equipment, machine tools, ships, rolling stock, German investments abroad, shares of industrial, transport, and other enterprises in Germany, etc.), these removals to be carried out chiefly for the purpose of destroying the war potential of Germany.

(b) Annual deliveries of goods from current production for a period to be fixed.

(c) Use of German labor.

3. For the working out on the above principles of a detailed plan for exaction of reparation from Germany an Allied reparation commission will be set up in Moscow. It will consist of three representatives—one from the Union of Soviet Socialist Republics, one from the United Kingdom, and one from the United States of America.

4. With regard to the fixing of the total sum of the reparation as well as the distribution of it among the countries which suffered from the German aggression, the Soviet and American delegations agreed as follows:

"The Moscow reparation commission should take in its initial studies as a basis for discussion the suggestion of the Soviet Government that the total sum of the reparation in accordance with the points (a) and (b) of the Paragraph 2 should be 22 billion dollars and that 50 percent should go to the Union of Soviet Socialist Republics."

The British delegation was of the opinion that, pending consideration of the reparation question by the Moscow reparation commission, no figures of reparation should be mentioned.

The above Soviet-American proposal has been passed to the Moscow reparation commission as one of the proposals to be considered by the commission. [. . .]

AGREEMENT REGARDING JAPAN

The leaders of the three great powers—the Soviet Union, the United States of America, and Great Britain—have agreed that in two or three months after Germany has surrendered and the war in Europe is terminated, the Soviet Union shall enter into war against Japan on the side of the Allies on condition that:

1. The status quo in Outer Mongolia (the Mongolian People's Republic) shall be preserved.

2. The former rights of Russia violated by the treacherous attack of Japan in 1904 shall be restored [. . .]

3. The Kurile Islands shall be handed over to the Soviet Union.

It is understood that the agreement concerning Outer Mongolia and the ports and railroads referred to above will require concurrence of Generalissimo Chiang Kai-shek. The President will take measures in order to maintain this concurrence on advice from Marshal Stalin.

The heads of the three great powers have agreed that these claims of the Soviet Union shall be unquestionably fulfilled after Japan has been defeated.

For its part, the Soviet Union expresses it readiness to conclude with the National Government of China a pact of friendship and alliance between the U.S.S.R. and China in order to render assistance to China with its armed forces for the purpose of liberating China from the Japanese yoke.

Joseph Stalin

Franklin D. Roosevelt

Winston S. Churchill

Further Reading

GENERAL REFERENCE

Israel, Fred L. *Student's Atlas of American Presidential Elections, 1789–1996*. Washington, D.C.: Congressional Quarterly Books, 1998.

Levy, Peter B., editor. *100 Key Documents in American History*. Westport, Conn.: Praeger, 1999.

Mieczkowski, Yarek. *The Routledge Historical Atlas of Presidential Elections*. New York: Routledge, 2001.

Polsby, Nelson W., and Aaron Wildavsky. *Presidential Elections: Strategies and Structures of American Politics*. 10th edition. New York: Chatham House, 2000.

Watts, J. F., and Fred L. Israel, editors. *Presidential Documents*. New York: Routledge, 2000.

Widmer, Ted. *The New York Times Campaigns: A Century of Presidential Races*. New York: DK Publishing, 2000.

POLITICAL AMERICANA REFERENCE

Cunningham, Noble E. Jr. *Popular Images of the Presidency: From Washington to Lincoln*. Columbia: University of Missouri Press, 1991.

Melder, Keith. *Hail to the Candidate: Presidential Campaigns from Banners to Broadcasts*. Washington, D.C.: Smithsonian Institution Press, 1992.

Schlesinger, Arthur M. jr., Fred L. Israel, and David J. Frent. *Running for President: The Candidates and their Images*. 2 vols. New York: Simon and Schuster, 1994.

Warda, Mark. *100 Years of Political Campaign Collectibles*. Clearwater, Fla.: Galt Press, 1996.

THE ELECTION OF 1932
and the Administration of Franklin D. Roosevelt

Badger, Anthony J. *The New Deal: The Depression Years, 1933–1940*. Chicago: Ivan R. Dee, 2002.

Cook, Blanche Wiesen. *Eleanor Roosevelt: Volume 2, The Defining Years, 1933–1938*. New York: Viking Press, 1999.

Davis, Kenneth Sydney. *FDR into the Storm, 1937–1940: A History*. New York: Random House, 1993.

———. *FRD the War President, 1940–1943: A History*. New York: Random House, 2000.

Fleming, Thomas. *The New Dealers' War: FDR and the War Within World War II*. New York: Basic Books, 2001.

Freidel, Frank. *Franklin D. Roosevelt: A Rendezvous With Destiny*. Boston: Little Brown, 1990.

Goodwin, Doris Kearns. *No Ordinary Time: Franklin and Eleanor Roosevelt: The Home Front in World War II*. New York: Simon and Schuster, 1994.

Kennedy, David M. *Freedom from Fear: The American People in Depression and War, 1929–1945*. New York: Oxford University Press, 1999.

Kyvig, David E. *Repealing National Prohibition*. Chicago: University of Chicago Press, 2000.

McJimsey, George. *The Presidency of Franklin Delano Roosevelt*. Lawrence: University Press of Kansas, 2000.

Pasachoff, Naomi E. *Frances Perkins: Champion of the New Deal*. New York: Oxford University Press, 2000.

Reynolds, David. *From Munich to Pearl Harbor: Roosevelt's America and the Origins of the Second World War*. Chicago: Ivan R. Dee, 2001.

Walch, Timothy, and Dwight M. Miller, editors. *Herbert Hoover and Franklin D. Roosevelt: A Documentary History*. Westport, Conn.: Greenwood Publishing Group, 1998.

INDEX

Numbers in **bold italics** refer to captions.

The EDITORS

ARTHUR M. SCHLESINGER JR. holds the Albert Schweitzer Chair in the Humanities at the Graduate Center of the City University of New York. He is the author of more than a dozen books, including *The Age of Jackson; The Vital Center; The Age of Roosevelt* (3 vols.); *A Thousand Days: John F. Kennedy in the White House; Robert Kennedy and His Times; The Cycles of American History;* and *The Imperial Presidency.* Professor Schlesinger served as Special Assistant to President Kennedy (1961–63). His numerous awards include: the Pulitzer Prize for History; the Pulitzer Prize for Biography; two National Book Awards; The Bancroft Prize; and the American Academy of Arts and Letters Gold Medal for History.

FRED L. ISRAEL is professor emeritus of American history, City College of New York. He is the author of *Nevada's Key Pittman* and has edited *The War Diary of Breckinridge Long* and *Major Peace Treaties of Modern History, 1648–1975* (5 vols.) He holds the Scribe's Award from the American Bar Association for his joint editorship of the *Justices of the United States Supreme Court* (4 vols.). For more than 25 years Professor Israel has compiled and edited the Gallup Poll into annual reference volumes.

DAVID J. FRENT is the president of Political Americana Auctions, Oakhurst, NJ. With his wife, Janice, he has assembled the nation's foremost private collection of political campaign memorabilia. Mr. Frent has designed exhibits for corporations, the Smithsonian Institution, and the United States Information Agency. A member of the board of directors of the American Political Items Collectors since 1972, he was elected to its Hall of Fame for his "outstanding contribution to preserving and studying our political heritage."